HEALEY'S WORLD

HEALEY'S

Denis Healey

WORLD

Travels with my camera

The Book Guild Ltd
East Sussex, England

First published in Great Britain in 2002 by
The Book Guild Ltd
25 High Street
Lewis, East Sussex
BN7 2LU

Designed by Derek Copsey Kate Copsey, Omnific Services

Printing and binding in Singapore under the supervision of
MRM Graphics Ltd, Winslow, Bucks

A catalogue record for this book is available from The British Library

ISBN 185776 672 5

Contents

Introduction

Until almost the middle of the nineteenth century, people could record the world as they saw it only by hand. Many travellers had learned enough about painting to record what interested them in watercolour. Charlotte Brontë painted Bolton Abbey and the moors around Haworth, and Goethe sketched the beauties of Italy.

The invention of daguerrotype led Delaroche to declare in 1842, 'From today, painting is dead' – an exaggeration, of course. But by the end of the nineteenth century, photography was regularly used to record people and places; in Britain, Emerson and Sutcliffe were outstanding. Before the First World War, Alex Keighley, who lived near my home in Yorkshire, won an international reputation for the landscape photographs he took all over Europe; it was he who taught me pastel painting when I was a schoolboy.

My father, a keen photographer himself, bought me my first camera, a Box Brownie IIa, in 1925. In 1936 I bought myself a vest-pocket Agfa to record my first journey abroad, when I cycled to Salzburg through Holland and Germany between leaving school and going to Oxford. I found it was invaluable when I cycled through France to the Pyrenees during my summer vacations, and even more so when I spent a month in Greece.

As a soldier in North Africa and Italy, I used it on the few occasions when I was able to take photographs – particularly at Anzio and, as the war ended, in southern Austria. Shortly after the war an American

Near the Dead Sea, Israel 1953

friend gave me my first 35mm camera, an Argus C-3, and photography began to be my passion. It blossomed in 1947 when I bought a single-lens reflex in Warsaw – an Exakta Varex IIa with a 2.8 Tessar lens. Twenty years later it became an enduring obsession when I acquired an Olympus 2 with a spot meter. In those days I developed and enlarged all my own photographs in a little boxroom at our house in Highgate.

In 1953 I got my first colour film and used it in Yugoslavia and Israel. Since then I have taken over 40,000 colour slides all over the world. Because my main political interest is international affairs, I have been lucky enough to travel on my work to Europe, Africa, the Middle East, Asia, the Soviet Union, China, North America, Mexico and the Caribbean – in fact, everywhere except South America. I never went without my camera.

Some of the greatest landscape photographers, such as Ansel Adams, prefer black and white; it is easier to produce an artistic photograph in black and white, since there are fewer variables to handle. Black and white is also better for photojournalism, as Cartier-Bresson demonstrates, since even the best colour film tends to appear slightly artificial in recording action in the real world. So I have continued to use black and white as well.

However, I rarely had time to search for the perfect composition during my political travels, and simply for recording a scene – or my family – I find colour superior, particularly since the film speeds available today are so much faster than the 10 ASA of my first Kodachrome.

I have organised this book in chapters covering places rather than in order of time.

Equator in Uganda

My Homes

I have been lucky to live for most of my life in beautiful parts of Britain. Though I was born in Kent at the end of the First World War, when my father was working as an engineer at Woolwich Arsenal, we moved to Yorkshire when I was five and my father became the head of Keighley Technical College. We then lived on the southern flank of Ilkley Moor. I often used to walk on the road over to Ilkley and later discovered that it was a favourite walking place for G. K. Chesterton, a hero of my youth, and his friend Father O'Connor from the Roman Catholic church in Keighley, who was the model for his detective Father Brown. When I mentioned this in my memoir, an old man wrote to me from Keighley to say that he used to walk as a boy with Father O'Connor along the same road. He told how, on one occasion, he accidentally made a rude noise; Father O'Connor simply said, 'An empty house is better than a bad tenant'.

On Saturday afternoons and Sundays I explored every beck and crag on the moors above us; I built dams with stones and tussocks of grass, and forced my body into rocky caves in the hope of finding hidden treasure. Our favourite walk took us over the moors through Keighley Gate to the escarpment overlooking Wharfedale from Bolton Abbey to Otley, which passes the prehistoric Swastika Stone to Windgate Nick. Then we went over the moors again, with a break to climb the Doubler Stones, and had tea at a farmhouse with paper-thin bread and butter and strawberry jam, before the last lap under Rivock

Ilkley Moor, Yorkshire

Edge back to Riddlesden. In front of us lay Airedale from the Druids' Altar above Bingley to the Pennine boundary between Yorkshire and Lancashire, which stretched in a great arc on the horizon from Oxenhope to Malham.

Looking across Keighley to the south we could just see the village of Haworth where the Brontës lived in the middle of the nineteenth century. Charlotte and Emily Brontë have always been among my favourite writers and I enjoy their books more every time I read them. Nothing expresses the essence of Yorkshire better than their novels *Jane Eyre* and *Wuthering Heights*, and the poems. In particular I love Emily's words:

I'll walk where my own nature would be leading,
It vexes me to choose another guide:
Where the grey flocks in ferny glens are feeding
Where the wild wind blows on the mountainside.

I was only five years old when my father took me to Malham Cove and Gordale Scar, my little brother on his shoulders, to marvel at the limestone cliffs. At that age I was less excited by the wrinkled white wall of the Cove than by the black streak on its surface, which my father told me marked the descent of Tom, the chimney sweep in *The Water Babies*. They are scarcely a mile apart – great limestone cliffs that have attracted poets and painters since the end of the eighteenth century. The Tate Gallery in London exhibits a magnificent painting of Gordale Scar by James Ward; I find the Scar particularly attractive in winter when the waterfalls are frozen. There is a typical grass track

Haworth Church, Yorkshire

from Gordale over the moor to Grassington in Wharfedale which allowed me to enjoy both Airedale and Wharfedale on my bicycle on the same day. Grassington was once a centre of the lead mining industry; in 1807 Edmond Keane and Harriot Mellon both performed in its Barn Theatre.

In all seasons the Dales keep their special beauty – summer when the bracken is green and sweet to smell, autumn when it is golden brown and the moors are flooded with purple heather, winter when all is white with snow and an icy wind makes eyes water. But loveliest of

Malham Cove, Yorkshire

Gordale Scar, Yorkshire

all is spring, when primroses stud the grey stone walls, the lush meadows are sprinkled with cowslips, and pools of bluebells glow luminous in the woods. And above all the larks, rising and falling in the pure sky: 'It was all Adam and maiden, and fire, green as grass' – Dylan Thomas's 'Fern Hill' captures exactly this part of my own childhood.

Above all I loved riding to Wharfedale and Bolton Abbey, a favourite subject of Turner and Girtin. It started as a priory founded by monks of the Dominican order. As so often they found a spot which was far from nearest town or village, where they could raise sheep and catch fish for their food. The stepping stones over which they crossed the Wharfe are still there, though recently restored. As a boy I once fell in the river which they crossed. Just above Bolton Abbey the Wharfe flows through a narrow crooked valley where it is squeezed between rocks and called the Strid. To jump across the Strid required courage as well as energy. Just above the Strid is the Valley of Desolation – so called because it was devastated by a fire. It was part of my favourite walk as a boy.

We would scramble through the beautiful woods by the Strid to Bolton Abbey. After eating our sandwiches on the grassy bank opposite the Abbey, while chaffinches fought over the crumbs, we would climb up the Valley of Desolation with its silvery waterfall, over a crag called Simon's Seat, and then race headlong down through the woods and fields and back to the Wharfe and Barden Tower – the ruin of an ancient castle built by Lady Anne Clifford.

The area has been irresistibly attractive to artists with brush and pen, from Wordsworth and Turner to the 'silent traveller' from China,

The Doubler Stones, Yorkshire

Chiang Yee, fifty years ago. John Ruskin celebrated its beauty unforgettably in *Modern Painters*: 'Up the valley the limestone summits rise, and that steeply, to a height of 1200 feet above the river which foams between them in the narrow and dangerous channel of the Strid. Noble moorlands extend above, purple with heather, and broken into scars and glens; and round every soft tuft of wood, and gentle extent of meadow, throughout the dale, there floats a feeling of this mountain power and an instinctive apprehension of the strength and greatness of the wild northern land. It is to the association of this

Bolton Abbey, Yorkshire

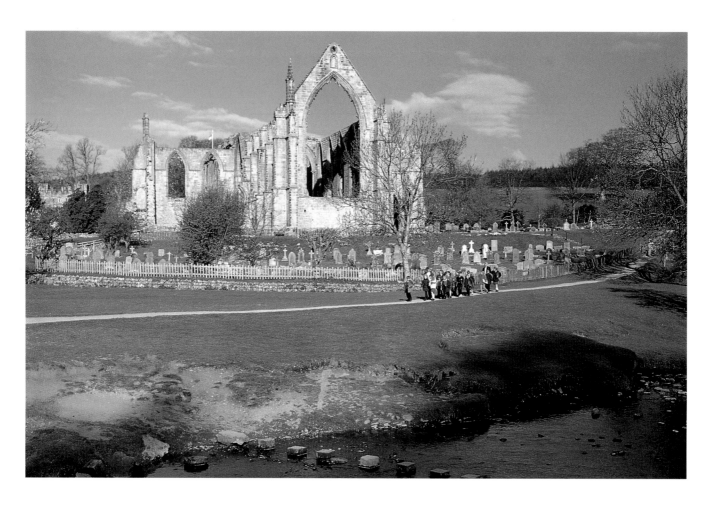

power and border sternness with the sweet peace and tender decay of Bolton Priory, that the scene owes its distinctive charm'. When I had to negotiate over the future of Rhodesia, one of its representatives, Michael Blundell, had lived close by as a boy.

While I was a student at Oxford, I knew a pretty girl called Edna Edmunds, whom many of us called 'Tomato Face' because she had such rosy cheeks. She was seen as the Zuleika Dobson of her day. During the war she came to teach in Keighley. The week before Christmas 1945, I left the army and we were married.

We had our honeymoon in a barn at Buckden in Upper Wharfedale – there were no rooms at the inn. The first night we were there, we were suddenly disturbed when the trap-door opened and an old lady holding a candle appeared with the words, 'I have brought some poetry to recite to you, would you like to hear it?' She did not interrupt any amatory exercises, however, because I had a painful boil at the bottom of my spine, which Edna had to bathe. The first morning we walked across the track to the inn into the dining room, and I clapped my hand to my back saying, 'Christ, my coccyx is painful'. Many of the old ladies, refugees from Leeds and Bradford, fainted; their knowledge of anatomy was no match for their imagination!

Since then we have returned many times to Burnsall, Grassington and other places in Upper Wharfedale. Perhaps the happiest occasion was when, as President of the National Trust Appeal for the Yorkshire Moors and Dales, I launched the appeal at Yockenthwaite – the source of the Wharfe. I accepted the area round Yockenthwaite as a present to the National Trust from Graham Watson; at the age of eighty, he had driven on his motorbike to Cambridge and back the day before he came to present Yockenthwaite to us.

After the war I spent six years in London as International

Overleaf:
Canal at Riddlesden, Yorkshire

Secretary of the Labour Party and then forty years as Member of Parliament for East Leeds. For most of our time in London we lived in Holly Lodge Gardens in what had been the estate of the Baroness Burdett-Coutts in the nineteenth century – the richest woman of her time and friend of the Duke of Wellington in his old age. She came to fascinate my wife, Edna; her career as a writer began with her biography of Angela Burdett-Coutts – 'Lady Unknown'.

Our house had a magnificent view from Highgate over the whole of London; on a clear day we could see the northern Downs on the horizon beyond St Paul's Cathedral. Our children loved it because it was so close to Hampstead Heath. I discovered later that it was on the edge of the road where John Betjeman lived as a child. I still find his poem 'Parliament Hill Fields' intensely moving:

… Soft the light suburban evening caught our ashlar-speckled spire,
Eighteen-sixty Early English, as the mighty elms retire
Either side of Brookfield Mansions flashing fine French-window fire.
Oh the after-tram-ride quiet, when we heard a mile beyond,
Silver music from the bandstand, barking dogs by Highgate Pond;
Up the hill where stucco houses in Virginia Creeper drown –
And my childish wave of pity, seeing children carrying down
Sheaves of drooping dandelions to the courts of Kentish Town.

Later we moved to a flat in St George's Square, Pimlico – an area of some literary interest, though it has been given a rather depressing image as the capital of Thomas Cubitt's stucco-land. I, however, loved its flowery gardens and its proximity to the Thames, the Tate Gallery and Chelsea.

I felt it essential to spend some of my time in the country, so we

Sussex Downs from Berwick

bought a small cottage just outside Withyham on the Kent/Sussex border. Our house at Withyham was a few miles from Oak Tree Cottage, where the poet William Butler Yeats lived for some years, with Ezra Pound as his secretary. Then we bought a larger house on the outskirts of Alfriston, in the Cuckmere Valley, with a wonderful view over Alfriston to the north, and down to Cuckmere Haven and the English Channel to the south. I chose Alfriston because the landscape, particularly the walk from Alfriston over to Jevington, where the ground is covered with heather and bracken, is very reminiscent of the

Yorkshire Dales. At Alfriston we were a few miles from the home at Rodmell of my other great literary idol, Virginia Woolf, and from Charleston Farm House where Virginia's sister, Vanessa, lived with Clive Bell and then with Duncan Grant, the painter.

I have learned to love the Sussex Downs as much as I love the Yorkshire Dales. The area near Alfriston, which includes Firle Beacon, fully justifies Kipling's description of 'our blunt, bow-headed, whale-backed, Downs':

Bare-sloped, where chasing shadows skim
And through the gaps revealed
Belt upon belt, the wooded, dim
Blue goodness of the Weald.

The village of Alfriston is one of the most beautiful in Britain. Its village green, called The Tye, faces its lovely church, often described as 'the cathedral of the Downs'. We particularly like to go there on May Day when the village children dance round the Maypole. Our favourite walk is from the hill overlooking the local town of Seaford, down to Hope Cove, where our children used to collect winkles and mussels; then along the cliffs to Cuckmere Haven, with a superb view of the so-called Seven Sisters – a series of chalk cliffs which run above the English Channel to Birling Gap. The whole area was notorious for smugglers – notably Jevington Jigg from the valley next to ours. Cuckmere Haven was also seen as a likely place for German spies to enter Britain during the two world wars.

The Seven Sisters, Sussex

Holidays

My first holidays were with my mother's family at Newnham-on-Severn in Gloucestershire, where my grandfather was station master at the tiny village halt. I loved the fresh salty air of the Severn Estuary and played with my brother on the tiny beach, which was more mud than sand. What I liked most of all was to walk up the hills behind Newnham to Pleasant Stile, which has one of the loveliest views in England. The great silver bend of the Severn lies below, with the Cotswolds blue on the horizon, Gloucester cathedral just visible on the left, and the little church of Newnham standing out against the river.

As a boy I first cycled to the Lake District and stayed in youth hostels from which I could climb the pinnacles of Langdale Pikes and the mountain of Helvellyn. I went several times to the Lake District after the war, partly to celebrate Wordsworth at his little home at Dove Cottage just outside Grasmere.

Our latest visit was in the spring of 2001 when the daffodils were out everywhere, and bluebells just beginning. Just south of Coniston are the country houses of Holker Hall, with a superb garden of azaleas and rhododendrons, and Levens Hall, with extraordinary topiary in which the trees are cut in geometrical shapes, reminiscent of the geometrical gardens at Jaipur in Rajasthan.

Newnham-on- Severn

Loch Lomond, Scotland

As a schoolboy I also cycled to Scotland over Shap Pass through Glencoe to Skye, where I stayed at the post office in Glen Brittle before climbing the Cuillins. T.S. Eliot described Glencoe beautifully in his poem:

Here the crow starves, here the patient stag
Breeds for the rifle. Between the soft moor
And the soft sky, scarcely room
To leap or soar. Substance crumbles, in the thin air
Moon cold or moon hot. The road winds in
Listlessness of ancient war,
Languor of broken steel,
Clamour of confused wrong, apt
In silence. Memory is strong
Beyond the bone. Pride snapped,
Shadow of pride is long, in the long pass
No concurrence of bone.

The base for our Polaris submarines was at Faslane near Loch Lomond, so I went there several times as Defence Secretary.

I found cycling in Scotland as a schoolboy extremely difficult and tiring; there were then no paved roads in the north-west Highlands, only sandy tracks covered with rocks and boulders. Today you tend to drive too fast on the macadam highways. But the countryside is as lovely as ever – heather-clad mountains, blue lakes and ferny wooded glens. I particularly love the approach to Skye by Loch Duich, with its little castle of Eilan Donan. The islands are all exceptionally beautiful – even the oddly-named Rum, Eigg and Muck. I was not surprised that John Smith chose the sacred island of Iona for his final

Overleaf:
Eilan Donan castle, Scotland

resting place after his tragically early death. The Gulf Stream keeps the water exceptionally warm round the Western Isles, so they are excellent for bathing.

I went several times to Cornwall for my summer holidays as a schoolboy, staying at Mawgan Porth. My favourite place was Bedruthan Steps – a long sandy cove studded with great rocks, one of which looks remarkably like Queen Elizabeth I. When our children were young we used to have our family holiday camping there. Later we would spend a week or so at Padstow in a little apartment above Rick Stein's superb fish restaurant, which has a terrace overlooking the bay. We have always preferred north-west Cornwall to the southern coast because it is less crowded and the beaches are superb, although nowadays in summer the narrow roads are usually chock-a-block with cars and caravans. But once off the road it is still the Cornwall so brilliantly described in the poems of John Betjeman:

We used to picnic where the thrift
Grew deep and tufted to the edge;
We saw the yellow foam-flakes drift
In trembling sponges on the ledge
Below us, till the wind would lift
Them up the cliff and o'er the hedge.
Sand in the sandwiches, wasps in the tea,
Sun on our bath-dresses heavy with the wet,
Squelch of the bladder-wrack waiting for the sea,
Fleas round the tamarisk, an early cigarette.

My Family at Bedruthan Steps, Cornwall

32

Ireland

My father was born in Ireland at Kiltyclogher, in County Leitrim, close to Enniskillen. His father had been a Fenian in his youth but, like so many Irish in the nineteenth century, had to go abroad for work. He settled in Todmorden, a typical mill town in Yorkshire on the border of Lancashire, when my father was a little boy.

I was immensely proud of my Irish ancestry and as a boy devoured my mother's *Celtic Myth and Legend*; before long Cuchulain, 'The Hound of Ulster', became my hero.

My favourite twentieth-century poet has always been Yeats. I was fascinated to discover that his family first settled in Ireland from Yorkshire in the seventeenth century. The Brontë family, of course,

My Grandfather's birthplace, Kiltyclogher

Kiltyclogher Fiddler

Turf-cutter, Connemara

were also Yorkshire-Irish, like me. There is some advantage is mixing Yorkshire muck with Irish magic.

It is surprising to see that the most famous fighters for Irish freedom were nearly all Protestant in faith, and often Anglo-Irish in origin – from Lord Edward Fitzgerald and Wolfe Tone two centuries ago, through Parnell to Yeats himself. Perhaps the most striking example is Maude Gonne, Yeats's first great love. She was the daughter of the brigade major of the British cavalry in Dublin, yet

Kinvarra, Galway

supported terrorism in the fight for Irish freedom. Her husband, John MacBride, was executed for his role in the Easter Rising, and after the Second World War I came to know his son, Sean.

I never met Yeats myself, but we often visited Penns in the Rocks where Yeats's friend, Lady Dorothy Wellesley, lived for some years. My room at Balliol College in Oxford looked across the Broad to the flat in which Yeats also lived for some time. In fact, he spent as much of his life in England as in Ireland – at the age of five he went to the Godolphin School in Hammersmith. In his later years he became an Irish senator, but his political candle burned with a very smoky flame – he was a great admirer of Mussolini and of the Irish proto-fascist, Kevin O'Higgins. His financial interests were legendary. He could read a balance sheet at a glance, and when a friend rang him up in 1923 to tell him he had been awarded the Nobel Prize for Literature, his only question was 'How much is it?'

Ireland has made a major contribution to English literature for the last two centuries, from Swift and Burke to Joyce and Beckett. Its dramatists include Goldsmith, Sheridan, Bernard Shaw, Synge and O'Casey. Despite my passion for Irish literature, I did not pay my first visit until 1969 when I was Defence Secretary. I had just set up the Ulster Defence Regiment to protect the Catholics in Belfast against persecution by its predecessor, the 'B' Special Police – an achievement for which I was rewarded years later. As I was walking by the river in Sligo, looking in vain for the Salley Gardens, someone rushed out of the public house across the road to present me with a bottle of Irish whiskey! Later, I visited Dublin a number of times to give lectures, and went to the Wexford Festival as a guest of Tony O'Reilly – an extraordinary man who, after playing rugby for Ireland twenty-nine times became Chief Executive of the Irish Milk Marketing Board and

created Kerry Gold, and then went to Pittsburgh to run the international H. J. Heinz Company.

I love Dublin especially; it is so full of historical and literary memories. There is a statue representing the River Liffey as a girl lying in a rippling stream of water, which the locals describe either as 'the floozy in the jacuzzi' or 'the hoor in the sewer'!

In 1995 Edna and I spent five weeks motoring round the island. We crossed from Swansea to Cork, then went down to Bantry across

Irish Girl

Irishmen, Bantry

The Healy Pass, Cork

the Healy Pass – not, alas, named after me! (Most of the Healys in Ireland come from the area around Cork). Then, after enjoying the beautiful landscapes of Connemara and the peninsulas of Kerry and Dingle, we drove up to Yeats's country. His famous patron, Lady Gregory, had lived at Coole Park; her beautiful home had been torn down for scrap under de Valera's government in 1941, but it was still possible to enjoy the lake which inspired Yeats' great poem 'The Wild Swans at Coole'. Even more exciting to me was to climb the tower at Thoor Ballylee where Yeats lived with his wife, George, and to see the room where he wrote much of his best poetry.

I took advantage of my political friendship with the diplomat David Gore Booth, to visit his ancestral home at Lissadell, an early Victorian mansion close to the sea in Drumcliff Bay. It has won immortal fame through Yeats' poem about his aunts Eva Gore Booth and Con Markiewicz:

The light of evening, Lissadell,
Great windows open to the south,
Two girls in silk kimonos, both
Beautiful, one a gazelle

Eva was a poet, feminist, socialist and pacifist. Her sister, Constance, married a Polish count to become Countess Markiewicz. She was condemned to death after the Easter Rising when she was commanding the rebels at St Stephen's Green.

On the way home we drove through Tipperary to the ruins of Cashel (once the capital of Munster) and gained some sense of medieval Irish history; St Patrick had preached there in AD 450, though the castle and cathedral were not built until AD 1169.

France

As a boy I saw France as a symbol of sophistication. I started my love affair with it by reading Voltaire's *Candide* and Rousseau's *Confessions*. Before long I read all the novels of Stendhal, Flaubert, Colette and Montherlant. They seemed to me to have an understanding of human nature far in advance of English novelists. As a schoolboy in Bradford I used to rush from school to the Church Bookshop to buy picture postcards of the French Impressionists, particularly Monet. I soon became equally enthusiastic about the work of Picasso and Matisse. As a student in Oxford just before the war, I established the New Oxford Art Society, and organised a show of Picasso's drawings and etchings. I have always regretted not buying one of his Minotaur etchings, which I could have got for £5. But to me in those days, £5 was like £1 million.

In June 1937 I set off with a friend from Oxford for a visit to the Pyrenees in a car he had bought for £10. It worked fairly well, though the water got into the oil from time to time. So I strapped my trusty Rudge Whitworth bicycle to the side as a lifeboat; it also gave me independence whenever I wanted to travel some of the way on my own. It was my first visit to France, and I loved everything about it: the people, the extraordinary variety of the landscape, the food and the drink. When we stopped for our first meal at a bistro, just south of Dieppe, I tasted for the first time *petit pois à la Francaise*. To a boy brought up in Yorkshire on large, hard peas, sometimes made more palatable by being turned into a mush, it was a revelation. In those days you could buy a litre of country wine for about a penny.

Paris from the top of Notre Dame

We spent a week at a farm in the Pyrenees above Mosset, near Prades, the home of the great cellist Pablo Casals. The English Quakers had settled two German refugees there, Pitt and Yves Krueger, who represented all that was best in the Germany of the Weimar Republic. Both were passionately interested in music; Yves had known Toscanini in the early 1930s and used to sing Bach's 'My Heart Ever Faithful' as she did the farmyard chores.

I spent two wonderful and exhausting days climbing alone in the snow-capped mountains of the Canigou, sleeping in the open in a mossy forest just below the summit. We went several times to the fishing port of Collioure , celebrated by generations of painters, and drank little cups of strong black coffee with a small tumbler of cognac in the village square.

On my way back I paid the first of many visits to the Louvre, the Orangerie, and the Petit Palais, and saw the overwhelming display of French art at the Paris Exhibition. During a special journey to Giverny, I climbed over the wall of Monet's garden to see the lily

Collioure, South of France

Fisherman at Collioure,
South of France

Overleaf:
Cagnes, South of France

ponds which he painted so often in his final years. He had died at Giverny only eleven years before. When I visited the gardens again fifty years later, they were open to the public and had been carefully replanted – one of the loveliest sights in Europe.

The next summer holiday I spent hitch-hiking round France with a friend and sampling the extraordinary variety of French youth hostels. One of the them in the Alps above La Grave, appropriately run by Les Amis de la Nature, had only one bed, 30 feet broad, on which everyone piled in together. Another, on the Cote d'Azur at St Raphael, was an old Roman theatre; we all slept on the floor of the stage under the stars.

After the war, when I was married, Edna and I would spend at least a week of every summer holiday in France. We both loved the French cabaret songs, many of which we heard either at the Olympia Music Hall or in the cabarets of Montmartre. Edith Piaf and Maurice Chevalier had long been favourites, but once we had heard Yves Montand he came first for both of us. We still often listen to records of him singing songs with words by the poet Jacques Prévert. His song 'Barbara' is the most moving reflection on the Second World War I know, and his rendering of songs of medieval France is incomparable.

From my schooldays I had been an obsessive film-goer. The so-called *films noirs* of Clouzot impressed me particularly and my favourite actor in those days was Jean Gabin, who was also a good singer. I still think the best comment on the idiocy of war is Renoir's film, *La Grande Illusion*, starring the German actor/director Erich von Stroheim.

Most summer holidays we would spend at least a week on the shores of Lake Annecy before going into the high Alps near Chamonix. Annecy itself is a beautiful little town where the lake

Students by the river Seine, Paris

Corsica

becomes a stream on its way to the river Rhône. There are magnificent walks in the surrounding hills. When our children were old enough, the whole family would camp in a field outside Talloires, from which Cézanne painted the castle of Duingt across the lake. We usually came home along the Riviera coast, calling at Vallauris, a village where Picasso lived; we were able to buy a lamp designed by him quite cheaply. Avignon, once the home of popes, and the ruins of Les Baux were another favourite. We sometimes went to the Pyrenees

The Pyrenees

through the medieval town of Carcassonne, which gave us a chance to

see the superb collection of Toulouse-Lautrec's paintings at his home in Albi.

When we had moved to Alfriston, we found it very convenient to spend a few days in Normandy, crossing on the ferry from Newhaven to Dieppe. We loved the coast from Etretat to Tréport and would invariably go from Rouen to see Monet's lily gardens at Giverny. The countryside of Normandy was particularly beautiful in the early summer, and we loved walking along the river near Les Andelys.

Inevitably, my interest in international affairs brought me in touch with French political leaders – from Léon Blum, head of the Popular Front in the 1930s, to Lionel Jospin, who is now Prime Minister. France had a tradition of state control, or *dirigisme*, which went back to Louis XIV and Colbert. Post-war French governments built on the pre-war Grandes Ecoles to establish a National School of Administration (ENA). This provided their senior civil servants with management and administrative training far superior to anything available in Britain. The omni-competence of these so-called *énarques* was legendary. My friend, Félix Baumgartner, for example, moved without difficulty from being Governor of the Central Bank, to Finance Minister, to head of the great chemical company, Rhône Poulenc, without abandoning his wide range of cultural interests, which included a close friendship with Sophia Loren and her husband, the film producer Carlo Ponti. Since de Gaulle, the *énarques* have provided many of the political leaders in all parties.

As a socialist, I found it difficult at first to admire de Gaulle. However, in recent years, I have come to regard him as one of the greatest European statesmen of the twentieth century. His memoirs are quite as good as those of his great rival, Winston Churchill. Throughout his life he was a modest human being. Edna and I were

The Cross of Lorraine,
near Colombey-les-Deux-Eglises

intrigued by his little home at Colombey-les-Deux-Eglises, and even more by the Cross of Lorraine which is planted in his memory in the hills nearby.

De Gaulle regarded Britain as America's Trojan Horse in Europe. Many French politicians have distrusted us for the same reason. So they have preferred Germany as a partner in building a united Europe, despite having fought against Germany in 1870 and in two world wars, and finding Germany much larger than France after its reunification.

Germany and Austria

In the summer holiday of 1936 between school and Oxford, I spent five weeks cycling through Europe to see Reinhardt's production of Goethe's *Faust* at the Salzburg Festival. Hitler had not been long in power, and since the Olympic Games were being held in Germany, the people were told to be nice to foreigners. So I was able to talk freely about politics even in the youth hostels, which were then full of *Hitler Youth*.

It was the best holiday of my life, and the cheapest. I slept in barns or the local youth hostels which in Germany then cost a penny a night and a penny for breakfast. So the whole five weeks cost me only £5 including the price of my passport, the fare from Harwich to Antwerp, my ticket to *Faust* and presents to take home.

Scarcely eighteen years had passed since the armistice which ended what was then still seen as Armageddon. Some of the Germans I met had fought in Belgium against France. One bitter Alsatian cried, 'A plague on both your houses'. The young Austrians were Nazi to a man. The Czechs were Socialist or Communist. Most of the Germans idolised Hitler, despised the French and Italians, and claimed to admire the British. Yet I also met many young Germans who were staunchly anti-Nazi; there were mainly working men who assured me that many of their friends simply wore brown shirts over their red shirts; they were called Beefsteaks – outside brown and inside red.

As a result, I have always found it impossible to hate the Germans as such, even during the war. After the war, I became friendly with many Germans. As International Secretary of the Labour Party I had

The Drachenfels from the British Embassy, Bonn

the leader of the Social Democratic Party of Germany, Kurt Schumacher, invited to Britain. I made many German friends at the Anglo-German conferences which were held every Easter in Koenigswinter, a small town on the Rhine at the foot of the Drachenfels; for example, General von Senger und Etterlin, who had commanded the German army at Cassino while I was a few miles north at Anzio. A tall cadaverous man, he was a lay priest of the Dominican order, and had now become headmaster of Salem, the experimental school which Kurt Hahn started before coming to Britain to found Gordonstoun, where Prince Philip was educated.

In my experience, private international conferences such as those of Koenigswinter, and those of the Bilderberg Group have a value in world affairs far greater than the well-publicised meetings of the United Nations, NATO or the European Union. The participants are able to talk more freely and to develop lasting personal friendships which lubricate the normal diplomatic channels. Moreover, such conferences can include businessmen, bankers, trade unionists and journalists who have no other means of learning about one another's problems.

My first visit to Berlin was just before the blockade ended in May 1949. I flew out from Schleswig in a Hastings aircraft loaded with coal, and back to Hamburg in a plane which had been carrying fish. I was redolent with the memory for some time.

The Social Democrats were the key to the strength of the western position in Berlin. Ernst Reuter, the Lord Mayor, was a man of exceptional wisdom and experience who knew the Communist strategy from first-hand experience – like many of my Social

Near the Wolfgang See

Democrat friends, including the brilliant journalist Rix Loewenthal, he had been a member of a small Communist faction in his youth. Willy Brandt, who later succeeded him as Lord Mayor, became one of my dearest friends for the rest of his life. My closest German friend, however, was Helmut Schmidt whom I met when he was a young senator from Hamburg. He was my age, had fought in Russia while I was fighting in Italy, and had come to very similar conclusions both about war and about the need for unity in Europe. We worked together in and out of government for thirty years.

Prince Ludwig's Palace, Hohenschwangau

I had always loved German music, particularly Bach and Beethoven, but did not begin reading German literature until after the war. My favourites were Goethe and Heine but I developed a taste for the novelists Fontana and Thomas Mann. Despite its savagery and pessimism, I love the literature, music and painting of the Weimar period – Brecht, Weill, Grosz and Dix.

Edna and I would spend a week in Germany most summers on our way to Italy through the Austrian Tyrol. We loved to discover little villages hidden in the depths of the Black Forest – I once managed to visit the great German philosopher, Albert Schweitzer, there. The mountains of Bavaria are given a unique attraction by the palaces built there by the mad Prince Ludwig at Neuschwanstein, Hohenschwangau and Linderhof.

My support for German rearmament inside NATO made me very unpopular in the Labour Party. Yet I was as surprised as everyone else in the western world when Gorbachev withdrew the Red Army from eastern Germany and allowed the two parts of Germany to unite again. Every western intelligence service had insisted that this was inconceivable. Mrs Thatcher was strongly opposed to German reunification, as was France. However, I was right in believing that a united Germany, far from being a threat to the West, would be its most powerful ally in Europe. I visited Berlin again just after reunification. It is the only time I have ever been in a city where everyone was smiling. The fall of the Berlin Wall was a symbol of how Gorbachev's vision could transform the world.

Austria played a key role in European politics from the Middle Ages until the end of the Second World War. Britain's King Richard the Lionheart was a prisoner in an Austrian castle when he was serenaded by Blondel. The Ottoman Empire reached the gates of

*Celebrating the end
of the Berlin Wall*

Vienna some centuries later. Napoleon slept in the Palace of Schoenbrunn after his defeat. The future of Europe was decided at the Congress of Vienna in 1815 where the Austrian Foreign Minister, Metternich, one of the cleverest politicians in history, played the leading role. Before long the Austro-Hungarian Empire stretched from southern Poland to Herzegovina in the south Adriatic, including

*The Brandenburg Gate
behind the Berlin Wall*

parts of northern Italy. Defeat in 1918 meant the end of the Hapsburg monarchy and in 1938 Hitler annexed Austria – with the agreement

of most of its people. However, Hitler, like his predecessor Bismarck, (who once described a Bavarian as something between an Austrian and a man) despised the Austrians. Defeat in 1945 and the neutrality imposed by the peace treaty gave Austria a new start as an independent country. I was lucky enough to know the socialist leaders who were then responsible for Austria's revival – Presidents Renner, Koerner and Schaerf.

From the end of the eighteenth century, Austria became the capital of music in Europe: Gluck, Haydn, Mozart, Beethoven, Brahms, Schubert and Mahler all did most of their work in Vienna. I have always found the annual music festival at Salzburg the most enjoyable in Europe. The lakes and mountains in the surrounding countryside are exceptionally beautiful. Most beautiful of all, however, is the Tyrol, south of Innsbruck, where the local people wear their traditional costume on all festive occasions. A few days in the cool fresh air of those meadows is an ideal preparation for the descent into the heat of northern Italy over the Brenner Pass.

Austrian valley

Italy

I fell in love with Italy during the war when I travelled from the south of Sicily to the Austrian frontier above Trieste. On the way I took part in assault landings in Calabria and at Anzio. Otherwise I was a staff officer at Bari in the heel of Italy, in Naples and Caserta, in Rome, Siena and Florence. In 1944 I saw the great explosion of Vesuvius near Naples and at night could watch the molten lava flowing red down the volcano's slopes. In Naples I made many lifelong friends. My colonel, Jack Donaldson, was as keen on music as I was. So we sought out the decrepit conductor of the San Carlo Opera Orchestra, Signore Baroni, and persuaded him to form a string quartet to give concerts for the forces. Jack's wife, Frankie, had a brilliant career in writing books. Her biography of her father, the playwright Freddy Lonsdale, is unique for combining cold objectivity with filial tenderness. Jack later became Minister of the Arts in the Callaghan government. When I was planning the landing at Anzio in the great baroque palace at Caserta, I saw Humphrey Bogart poking his head round a door during a visit to entertain the American forces.

My time at Siena gave me a chance to explore the beauties of Tuscany. On one expedition I went to Montegufoni to see the Italian home of the Sitwells. I was let into the drawing room. A shaft of sunlight illuminated Botticelli's *Primavera* – it was one of the most exciting moments in my life. I had not known that Montegufoni was

San Vigilio, Lake Garda

Lago di Carezza

Capri

used to store the best paintings from the Uffizi Gallery in Florence for the duration of the war.

The armistice in Italy was signed on 1 May 1945. I decided to make a final 'swan' and to get, if possible, into Austria and Yugoslavia. My driver and I left Florence in our jeep on the evening of 6 May to cross the Apennines over the Futa pass. Next day we drove up the Tagliamento Valley into Austria. It was another world – great grey precipices, silky waterfalls, turf green and soft, enamelled with cowslips and mountain flowers, peaks glistening with snow. Coming down the pass towards us were thousands of refugees of every nationality – Russians, Serbs, Poles, Italians – dressed in every possible way, doggedly tramping into Italy.

On the way back from Klagenfurt in lower Austria I went to Venice, which was already full of troops on day leave. I then drove back to my headquarters in crippling heat through Ferrara and Bologna.

Once the war was over, Edna and I were married – on 21 December 1945. Though we had enjoyed our honeymoon at Buckden, in the Yorkshire Dales, I thought we must have a second honeymoon in Italy. So in April 1946, after visiting the socialists in northern Italy with Harold Laski, Edna and I went to have a second honeymoon in Capri. At that time the island was full of families from Naples celebrating the Easter holiday by singing, accompanied by guitars and accordions.

On a later visit to Italy I went to see the Pope with a trade unionist from Lancashire, Bob Openshaw, and had my first chance to see the beautiful gardens behind the Vatican. Our interview with the Pope was unusual. It started with the Pope saying: 'I understand, Mr Openshaw, that you are a member of the National Executive Committee of the British Labour Party: you have a great responsibility.'

'Aye, Pope, and so have you,' replied Bob.

Overleaf: Abrruzzi

Malcesine, Lake Garda

It ended with the Pope opening a drawer in his desk and saying: 'I know you are not Roman Catholic yourself, Mr Openshaw, but perhaps you have friends who are. I have rosaries here – some black and some white. Which would you prefer?'

'Oh, I reckon I'll have one of each,' replied Bob. And so he did. And so did I.

Italy since then has always been our favourite country for holidays. We would spend a week in the mountains – either the Alps round Aosta, or the Dolomites round Fié above Bolzano. Then we would have a week

by the lakes — either Garda or Maggiore. Before long our favourite destination became Bellagio at the northern end of a narrow peninsula in Lake Como. The Rockefeller Foundation in New York had made the Villa Serbelloni in the woods above Bellagio a centre for international seminars, at which I used to lecture. It was there that I first met Condoleeza Rice, a black woman who is now President Bush's National Security Adviser. I wrote much of my memoir, *The Time of My Life*, in a monk's cell overlooking the eastern part of the lake.

On the whole, however, I most love Tuscany. It combines beautiful landscape with great paintings and sculpture. Florence, its capital, has no rival in the world for architecture and works of art, except perhaps Isfahan in Iran. Yet Siena and San Gimignano, though smaller, have the same quality. The greatest Sienese painting dates from the early Renaissance and is unique in its use of pale green and pink. San Gimignano is remarkable for the number of its square towers, which dominate the landscape for miles around.

As International Secretary of the Labour Party after the war, I became deeply involved in Italian politics, trying to unite the socialist parties with little success: I started with two parties and finished with five. I came to know some of the Italian writers well, particularly Ignazio Silone, who had a beautiful Irish wife called Darina, and Alberto Moravia. Italian films have also been among my favourites, particularly *The Bicycle Thieves*, a film made by Rossellini about poverty in Milan just after the war, and *Il Postino*, a beautiful film about a postman who travelled all over Capri by bicycle.

Several Italian towns hold annual festivals to celebrate their Renaissance. My favourite is the Palio, held in the town hall square of Siena, which is shaped like a scallop shell — a horse race is run in fifteenth century costume. A similar festival is held in Urbino. The

Festival at Urbino

festival in Venice is particularly remarkable because it takes place on the water as well as in the main piazza.

When visiting Venice we love to stay at Asolo in the hills to the north, in the Villa Cipriani. On one occasion we had the good luck to meet Freya Stark, one of the last great women explorers, who made her name as the first European to discover the Hadramaut – a sunken valley south of the Arabian desert, which I had the good fortune to visit myself as Defence Secretary.

Despite the enormous increase in tourism, Venice remains one of the loveliest cities in the world, particularly during its annual festival in late winter. It has a group of beautiful islands offshore. Burano and Murano are remarkable for the bright colours of their houses. Edna and I prefer Torcello, the monastery of which is surrounded with beautiful gardens. Ruskin also loved it.

Festival, Venice

Switzerland and the Alps

Switzerland in Europe, like Singapore in South-East Asia, is an extraordinary example of how a small state can achieve economic and social miracles despite belonging to no regional organisation. Like Singapore, it has a mixed population, yet the French, Germans and Italians have lived in complete harmony there for the last 150 years, though France, Germany and Italy have frequently fought one another. Switzerland's federal democracy and racial harmony are a model for the world. Its landscape has provided inspiration for generations of writers and painters.

When I was the young International Secretary of the Labour Party after the war, I found that the Swiss ambassadors in London, because their country was committed to neutrality, were my best source of objective information on what was going on in the rest of Europe.

Though we spent many summer holidays in Switzerland we did not discover the beautiful lakes above St Moritz until fairly late in life. In recent years we have preferred the area round the lakes of Silvaplana and Sils to other parts of Switzerland. They lie in a high open valley which ends in the little hamlet of Maloja, almost on the Italian frontier. The German philosopher Nietzche lived at Sils-Maria for the last years of his life, and the Italian-born painter, Segantini, spent most of his life painting Alpine scenery near his home in Maloja: there is a superb exhibition of his work in a gallery at St Moritz.

The best-known of the Alps, Mont Blanc, is in France, close to the

Mountains above Talloires

Swiss frontier. The little town of Chamonix at its foot is the best base for exploring it. Two of the loveliest Alpine peaks – Monte Rosa and the Matterhorn – are best approached from Aosta in Italy. The Italian national park of Gran Paradiso below Monte Rosa is well worth visiting for its mixture of beautiful flowers and unusual animals.

Switzerland itself is as famous for its lakes as for its mountains. Lake Constance forms the border between Switzerland and Germany. Lake Lucerne contains a small peninsula of woods and mountains called Bürgenstock which I visited frequently for meetings of international politicians. Lake Geneva, on the frontier with France, is notable for many reasons. The French writer Voltaire chose to retire to Ferney on its outskirts. There are superb art galleries in Geneva, Zurich and Winterthur which exhibit unique collections of Impressionist painters and of German and Swiss artists.

Despite having four distinct populations speaking French, German, Italian and Romansh, the Swiss declared themselves an independent state during the Middle Ages and William Tell became their symbol of the fight for independence. Switzerland committed itself to neutrality during the Reformation, and in 1815 the Congress of Vienna agreed that it should be permanently neutral. It has made good use of its neutrality to assist peace-making throughout the world. In 1863, the Swiss, Jean-Henri Dunant set up the Red Cross. During the Second World War, Allied prisoners who escaped from Germany and Italy found Switzerland a reliable haven.

The right to call a referendum is given to the Swiss people as a whole, although each of the national assemblies of its twenty-two cantons has its own constitution and legislative body. Federal laws are drafted by a college of seven members, the Federal Council. However, if within ninety days after a decision by the Assembly, signatures can

Edna on Mont Blanc

Above Fie

Lake of Sils

Painter, Montenvers

be obtained from 30,000 active citizens, the whole people are called upon to decide whether a law should be finally accepted or rejected. This is the 'Right of Referendum'. The wording of a referendum needs choosing with great care to avoid prejudicing its outcome. I recall a priest in the Valais quoting an example: 'Should you smoke while reading the missal?' and 'Should you read the missal while you are smoking?' invite opposite answers though they appear to mean the same.

The Swiss people also have the right to initiate legislation. Thus, 50,000 active citizens may demand an amendment of the articles of the constitution, or the adoption of new articles. No other democracy in the world gives so much direct expression to the popular will. However, since the late 1970s fewer than half the Swiss have bothered to vote in parliamentary debates, and they have by far the lowest average voting turnout in Europe. So there are limits to Switzerland's role as a model for the European Union as a whole.

All Swiss citizens serve their country for four months at the age of 20 and then twenty days a year until the age of 36. A Swiss soldier keeps all his equipment at home, not only his uniform but his rifle, ammunition and sometimes even his motorcycle or jeep.

Three-fifths of Swiss territory is Alpine and it includes 772 square miles of glacier, so it has an irresistible appeal to a photographer.

Greece

No flushful tint the sense to warm –
Pure outline pale, a linear charm.
The clear-cut hills carved temples face,
Respond, and share their sculptural grace.

Tis Art and Nature lodged together,
Sister by sister, cheek to cheek;
Such Art, such Nature and such weather,
The All-in-All seems here a Greek.

Herman Melville

As an undergraduate at Oxford I studied Latin, Greek, ancient history and philosophy. A travelling exhibition from Balliol gave me the whole of July 1939 for my first visit to Greece. Everywhere I was conscious of the approaching war. In fact I was briefly arrested as a German spy at Eleusis; some little boys saw me taking photographs and, as I was wearing shorts, assumed I was a member of the *Hitler Youth*!

In Athens I stayed on the lower slopes of Lycabettus at the British School – an institution for postgraduate archaeologists. Most of its members were very upper class, with names such as Camilla, Lesbia, Sergei and Cosmo. One, however, was a down-to-earth New Zealander, Tom Dunbabin, who later helped to organise the Greek resistance in Crete.

Evzones on the Acropolis

Then I travelled on foot or by bus to Corinth and round the Peloponnese. I was fascinated by the contrast between the friendly pragmatic peasants and the flashy corrupt townspeople I had met in Athens. At Mycenae, where I visited the Palace of Agamemnon, I stayed at a small hotel called 'Beautiful Helen', and my guide was called Aristotle. It was impossible to avoid memories of the classical world.

Many of the people I met had emigrated to the United States, and returned to visit their relatives. I remember particularly one who had spent twenty-five years as a boxing promoter. He spoke the only East Side slang I have heard off the movies. Tilting back in his chair and leaning a handsome, rugged, stubbled face on his stick, a crepe-banded straw hat on his head, he told me about his life there.

There were few roads in those days, so I had to walk over the Taygetus mountains to get from Sparta to Kalamata. Then I went to Olympia, which gave its name to the Olympic Games, and took a boat across the Gulf of Corinth to Itea. Driving from there up to Delphi was a wonderful experience. It was dark, the stars shone brilliantly and the sky was full of falling lights. Delphi, way up in the mountains, looked like a net of stars. As we drove up, the headlights tunnelling through the ghostly olive trees, the children on the bus sang popular songs.

Delphi has ever since been one of my favourite haunts, combining beautiful landscape, ruined temples and superb sculpture. From Delphi I went mainly by foot to the ancient monastery of Hosios Loukas (St Luke), then by foot over the mountains to Thebes and by train to Athens.

Delphi

I prepared for my journey round the Aegean islands by going to the promontory of Sunium, where a beautiful temple overlooks the sea. My favourite island was Mykonos with its great medieval windmills. Nowadays mass tourism has reduced its appeal; I prefer Santorini – the summit of a volcano which has sunk into the sea, where the middle of the crater floats below like a black fried mushroom.

As the Labour Party's International Secretary after the war, I went back to Athens several times for conferences, which gave me a chance to visit areas hitherto unknown to me. Most impressive was Meteora, where a broad valley is punctuated by great pillars of stone whose peaks were chosen by medieval priests as the safest place to build their monasteries. By far the most interesting monastery today, however, is Vatopaidi on Mount Athos in the peninsula of Khalkhidiki in northern Greece, which I visited a few years ago – to be greeted by one of the monks in broad Yorkshire!

In the spring Greece produces a mass of wild flowers over the most stony and dry of its fields. Of all of them I most love the asphodel, which pokes up its little leaves and buds through the tiniest cracks in the marble floors of ancient monuments. Most dazzling, however, are the avenues of daphnie – a laurel with white or scarlet flowers against dark green leaves.

For the last twenty years I have spent a week or more every summer in Crete, where a Cretan friend of mine, Minos Zombanakis, organises a seminar of bankers, businessmen, academics, journalists and politicians from Europe, North America and Japan, to discuss world affairs.

Crete has always regarded itself as separate from Greece. Indeed, it is as close to Libya as to Athens. Its history goes back at least 3,000

Overleaf: Mykonos

Edna at Sunium

years to the Minoan civilisation, which produced the palaces of Knossos, Phaistos and Malia. Homer and Hesiod say that Zeus, the king of the gods, who was born in Crete on Mount Ida, abducted a Phoenician princess and took the form of a bull to swim with her on his back to Crete – giving her name – Europa – to our continent. Europa gave birth to three sons, one of whom (Minos) lived at Knossos. Personally, I feel Sir Arthur Evans, who excavated Knossos, did too much unreliable restoration there.

Evening at Santorini

Monastery at Meteora

Crete was occupied successively by the Phoenicians, Romans, Turks and Germans, achieving a stable freedom only after the Second World War. The island has achieved fame since classical times. The Cretan painter Domenikos Theotocopoulos went to Spain and won worldwide recognition as El Greco. The eleventh-century Arkadi monastery, overlooking a wild gorge on the edge of a lonely plateau, was the site of a tragic incident in 1866 when a thousand Cretan refugees decided to blow themselves up rather than surrender to the Turks. During the Second World War, British agents organised effective armed resistance in Crete against the German occupation. Several have written good books about their experiences, though I prefer *The Cretan Runner* by Psychoundakis.

Rethymnon offers an attractive mixture of Venetian and Turkish architecture; Khania has a quiet quay where you can sip ouzo with your coffee and watch the passing throng. The Gorge of Samaria is one of the most exciting in the world. You can walk down to the sea in five hours — if you are young and strong.

Crete

Mediterranean Islands

Crete and the islands in the Aegean Sea are best seen as part of Greece for their landscape and culture. The other islands of the Mediterranean are each unique, with a history of occupation by foreign powers which is reflected in their architecture.

As a soldier I landed in Sicily from Tunisia and was delighted to find myself in Europe again. My favourite spot has always been Taormina, a rocky balcony above the sea with a stupendous view across the ancient Greek theatre to the volcano of Mount Etna. The Aeolian Islands, north of Sicily, are mainly volcanic – Stromboli is the most impressive and is often in eruption.

In the 1960s, as Defence Secretary, I visited our bases in Cyprus and Malta several times. Cyprus is the more attractive. Lying only forty miles from Turkey and sixty miles from Syria, its strategic importance led to occupation by the Hittites, the Persians, the Egyptians and the Greeks.

During the Crusades, Richard the Lionheart conquered the island to liberate his fiancée, Berengaria of Navarre; she was crowned Queen of England in Cyprus at Limassol. Richard sold Cyprus to the Knights Templar and they then sold it to the Franks, who occupied it for 300 years until the Venetians took over. The Turks then held it for another three centuries. After the Second World War the Turks occupied the northern coast, though the bulk of its population speaks Greek and has often sought union with Greece – particularly when Archbishop

Girl in Cyprus

105

Markarios was their head, and Britain was their colonial power. So, while our air bases were mainly concerned with the Soviet threat during the cold war, and our naval forces were there to protect our trade routes to Asia, our soldiers there were mainly concerned to contain the risk of civil war between north and south.

The whole island is beautiful – the goddess Venus is said to have been born on one of its southern beaches. Personally, I love the northern coast best, particularly the Monastery of Bellapaix, overlooking the sea under rocky mountains.

Lindos

Rhodes is another beautiful island, especially in its mountainous interior. About 4000 years ago it was already trading with the Middle East, Egypt and Italy. In the third and second centuries BC, it was the biggest maritime power in the Mediterranean and produced some exceptional sculpture, such as the Laocoon Group and the Aphrodite of Rhodes; the world famous Colossus of Rhodes which once straddled the entrance to the harbour is unfortunately now no more.

In AD 1306 Rhodes was the base for the Lords of the Knights of St

John and served as an advanced bastion for the Christians against the Turks, who later occupied it. In 1911 the Italians took it from the Turks. The Germans occupied it in the last two years of the Second World War and in 1948 the British gave it to Greece.

I first visited Rhodes just as General Galtieri was occupying the Falklands in early 1982, and had just time to visit the lovely little peninsula of Lindos before returning to debate the Falklands in the House of Commons.

Corsica is an exceptionally beautiful island. Its coast has some interesting ports, but the interior is much more attractive. Its high craggy mountains are clothed with forests and flowery meadows, where the streams flow cool and clear – perfect for bathing. Some of its valleys host tall eucalyptus trees which must have come from Australia some time in the nineteenth century. In ancient times it was occupied by Greeks, Etruscans, Italians and Carthaginians, and later it was invaded by Vandals, Lombards and Saracens, as well as the Italian city states Pisa and Genoa.

Corsica lies a hundred miles south of the French coast and its people speak French, though its great national hero, Pasquale Paoli, who brought independence in 1875, was Italian in origin. France finally annexed the island in 1769 and its greatest novel, *Colomba*, was written by Prosper Merimée, the author of *Carmen*. The clan warfare described in *Colomba* reminded me of the American Wild West.

Sardinia lies just south of Corsica, but its people speak Italian, though in the past it suffered occupation by the people who also occupied its northern neighbour. I visited its north-east coast several times as the guest of my Saudi friend, Sheikh Yamani. The Emerald

Corsica

Coast, as it is called, is very beautiful; its wooded inlets offer perfect bathing beaches.

Malta was Britain's most important base in the western Mediterranean, so I went there several times as Defence Secretary. While its harbour has historical attractions, I prefer its capital, Medina, and the bathing beaches to the north.

The Balearic Islands off the eastern coast of Spain are major haunts of tourism. As usual, their most attractive areas are inland, away from the coasts, with a landscape of wooded hills.

All these islands share the warm seas of the Mediterranean, coloured from dark blue to pale emerald. So I would spent much of my time there on their beaches.

Fisherman, Malta

Spain and Portugal

In its early years, Spain was occupied by much the same invaders as the Mediterranean islands, but its most lasting foreign influence came from the Moors of North Africa. I have made several visits to Spain, mainly for conferences. The first was to Madrid and the towns which surround it – Avila, Segovia and Toledo. Avila is notable mainly for its medieval walls which the Moorish prisoners of King Alfonso VI took nine years to construct. Toledo is famous above all as the place where El Greco settled at the end of the sixteenth century, and painted his great view of the town. Nowadays Toledo is remembered for the siege of its fortress, the Alcazar, during the Spanish Civil War in 1936.

Spain's greatest painters were Velázquez and Goya, whose engravings *The Disasters of War* are a searing indictment of war as such. At the end of his life Goya became deaf and painted some of the most astounding pictures in history, notably *Satan Devouring His Children*.

In the twentieth century Spain's best painters (Pablo Picasso and the surrealist Salvador Dali) came from Catalonia on its frontier with south-eastern France, which has a regional identity very different from the rest of Spain. The extraordinary Temple of the Holy Family in Barcelona by its local architect, Antonio Gaudi, is his greatest work.

The most remarkable collection of pictures in Spain (and one of the world's greatest) is at the Prado museum in Madrid. Apart from its magnificent Spanish paintings, it also has one of the best collections

The Alhambra

Gaudi Cathedral, Barcelona

The Alhambra

by Flemish and German painters, notably Hieronymus Bosch, Breughel the Elder, Rubens, Dürer and Cranach. No one who loves art should miss it.

My favourite part of Spain, however, is Andalucia at its southern tip, which was occupied by the Moors for seven centuries until 1492; they made Cordoba the capital of the western Islamic empire. The orange and lemon trees add sparkle with their fruit and blossom to a region which is exceptionally beautiful, though nowadays the Costa del Sol from Malaga to Gibraltar is overcrowded with holiday beaches.

Only a few miles inland, however, there are beautiful white towns such as Ronda and Arcos, and above all the Alhambra of Granada – best visited in the spring when there is still snow on the mountains to the north.

The royal palace of the Alhambra was built by the Moorish king, Mohammed V, and then occupied for a time by Fernando and Isabella after their conquest of Grenada. In the nineteenth century the American writer, Washington Irving, gave it international fame through his romantic *Tales of the Alhambra*, which he wrote in the

empty rooms of the palace. While the Alhambra itself is a complex of beautiful Moorish buildings, the gardens and summer palace of the Generalife just across the valley are also exceptional, with a cypress grove and a staircase with water flowing down its balustrades. Albaicin is a Moorish village opposite the Alhambra – attractive but very steep to climb.

Cordoba to the north contains the most beautiful Moorish mosque in Spain, the Mezquita. The columns inside are striped red and white with alternate rings of brick and stone. Further down the River Guadalquivir, the architects of Seville also demonstrate its past with a Moorish minaret crowning the Christian cathedral. Spain's great dance, the flamenco, was invented in Seville – flamenco is an incomparable attraction of this region, with man and woman celebrating their sex to the sound of guitar and singing.

Spain looks east to the Mediterranean and south towards Moorish Africa. Portugal has always looked west to the Atlantic, and from the south Atlantic to black Africa and Asia, where it occupied many territories from Guinea and Mozambique to Macao and Timor.

In 1984 I spent a week sightseeing in Portugal. Its western coast is full of memories of its great explorers such as Vasco da Gama and King Henry the Navigator. The rocky cliffs of Capo de Rocca are the western tip of the European continent. I found Portugal's ancient capital, Sintra, near Lisbon, very interesting, though the nearby castle of Pena is too much an imitation of Ludwig of Bavaria's Neuschwanstein. Lisbon itself was overcrowded; its election did not seem to have aroused much enthusiasm. For me the most attractive area, as in Spain, was in the south – the Algarve next to Andalucia, with good beaches along its rocky coast and superb seafood. I flew back to London from Faro loaded with Portuguese ceramics.

The Low Countries

I had cycled through the Low Countries on my way to Germany when I went to Salzburg in 1936, and came to know them well through many visits after the war. My first journey abroad as International Secretary of the Labour Party was to Amsterdam, where the Dutch Social Democratic Labour Party was holding a conference to eliminate the phrase 'Social Democratic' from its title so as to signal its break with its Marxist past in the hope of attracting Roman Catholic voters. In fact the Catholic hierarchy threatened to excommunicate any of its flock who voted for the new Labour Party.

The leaders of the Labour Party were fine men such as Koos Vorrink, who had worked in the resistance until caught and put in a concentration camp. Five of the ministers in the post-war government had been in Buchenwald together.

Later Edna and I had a wonderful holiday motoring round the Zuider Zee where the people of each town wore their own version of the Dutch national dress, and the scenery was unique in its combination of canals, cows and windmills. The grass was shining green, the sky a powdery blue with a handful of tiny white clouds, the buds bursting on the trees with here and there an explosion of blossom. We remember Sloten in particular – calves wandering on the grass in front of incredibly spruce little houses, a windmill turning lazily above the blue canal, everything fresh and clean like a child's picture book. We also went to Amsterdam and The Hague to see their magnificent art galleries.

Canal in Holland

Lacemaker, Holland

In 1954 I attended the first meeting of an Anglo-American conference at the Bilderberg Hotel near Arnhem, which gave its name to the most valuable international gathering I have known. We chose Prince Bernhard of the Netherlands as our chairman because his political objectivity was above suspicion. He lived in a simple palace at Soestdijk nearby, and his daughter Beatrix (later to become queen) acted as the conference secretary.

One of my best friends has always been Wim Duisenberg, whom I first knew as the Dutch Finance Minister when I was Chancellor of the Exchequer. As head of the European Central Bank, he is now one of the most influential men in Europe, famous for his great shock of white hair. On returning from the United States, he once dropped in on me with a present for my son, Tim. It was a steel catapult which fired steel ball bearings about as large as marbles – one of the most lethal weapons I have ever known.

I soon came to know Belgium better, since I was the London

Palace of Soestdijk

correspondent of the socialist newspaper *Le Peuple* and a close friend
of its editor, Victor Larock. The post-war leader of the Belgian
Socialist Party, Louis de Brouckère, was a mathematician of world
standing. He had helped to found the Second International before the
First World War, and when I knew him was tall and erect at eighty,
with a long white beard, twinkling eyes and a penetrating intellect.

Belgium was divided between its Flemish population on the coast
of the North Sea and its French speaking population inland; their
differences might well have provoked a civil war had it not been for the
efforts of Paul Henri Spaak, later to become NATO's Secretary General.

Though I was to spend much of my time in Brussels, where both
NATO and the European Community had headquarters, I never found
that city very exciting – unlike my Yorkshire/Irish heroine, Charlottë
Brontë, who fell in love with her tutor there when she was learning
French. Nevertheless, the little statue of Manneken-Pis has always
attracted me for portraying the innocence of childhood. Bruges,
however, I find one of the most attractive towns in the world, with its
network of canals and beautiful churches.

The Low Countries are also remarkable for the number of great
painters they have nourished, starting with Van Eyck, who may be
said to have invented oil painting. My favourites are Breughel,
Rembrandt and Vermeer.

Luxembourg is always described as one of the Low Countries,
although it is little more than a town built on a wooded cliff inland.
Politically and economically it is for practical purposes part of
Belgium, although it has always maintained a separate defence
identity.

Bruges

Scandinavia

Scandinavia has always attracted me as a politician for the achievements of its pragmatic social democracy. I was the London correspondent of the Norwegian Labour Party newspaper, *Arbeiderbladet* from 1946 until I became Defence Minister in 1964. Its editor, Martin Tranmael, was a man of demonic energy who had been a close friend of the Russian Bolshevik, Bukharin – indeed, the Norwegian Labour Party itself joined the Comintern for several years after the First World War. The secretary of its Labour Party, Haakon Lie, used to tell me that if the Norwegians had had another hundred men at the Battle of Stamford Bridge, half the world would now be speaking Norwegian!

As Defence Secretary, I made my first visit to Norway in 1964. Its Defence Minister, Gubbe Harlem, was a close friend. His daughter, Gru Harlem-Bruntland, became Prime Minister in the 1980s and is now the United Nations' High Commissioner for Refugees.

Edna and I flew one Friday in April 1965 to Norway for a weekend in the Arctic Circle. We started in Tromsö, where we dined in the home of a local councillor. It was like straying onto the set of a play by Ibsen – the claustrophobic nineteenth-century furniture with aspidistras and heavy curtains, the mayor with his pretty young wife, the bishop and the army officers. The next morning we flew up the coast, scaring herds of reindeer over the snowy tundra, to visit airfields, underground headquarters and artillery positions in the far

North Cape, Norway

Church, Bergen

north, where British forces made regular use of the winter warfare training school.

I have always loved Henrik Ibsen — his plays are brilliant in their understanding of the power element both in politics and personal life. My favourite Norwegian artist, Edvard Munch, is very different — one of the first and best Expressionist painters.

Iceland, on the edge of the Arctic Circle, is a country of glaciers and volcanoes, so it is sparsely populated. Yet it produced the first

Bodo, Norway

democratic parliament in the craggy hills of Thingvellir. Wystan

Stockholm, Sweden

Auden and Louis MacNeice wrote an excellent book about their voyage to Iceland. I myself made a visit in 1994 and found both the land and the people exceptionally attractive. Surprisingly, most of the immigrants to Iceland come from Japan.

Norway has always looked west across the sea to Britain, the United States and Canada. Sweden, however, looks east towards Russia and Finland and south towards Germany. It is easy to forget that it once had a great empire which included parts of Germany and Russia as well as Norway and Finland. Now it is remarkable for the prosperity it has achieved through half a century of social democracy.

Stockholm itself has some excellent modern buildings – notably the town hall – but I prefer the countryside with its little wooded islands and peninsulas such as Saltsjobaden, which I visited several times for conferences. Sweden's great dramatist, Strindberg, was a neurotic pessimist: 'Why does he hate me, I have never helped him?' is one of my favourite quotations. Yet Stockholm's best artist was the illustrator Carl Larsson, who produced inimitable watercolours of a normal Swedish family. Sweden's great sculptor, Carl Milles, is well represented in and around the city.

Finland is fascinating in many ways. Its ambassador in London after the war, Eero Wuori, was a close friend; he later became Foreign Minister, yet he had fought in the Finnish Red Army as a general in 1917. In Sibelius, Finland produced one of the greatest composers of our time. His great memorial in the woods outside Helsinki is well worth a visit. In summertime Finland's countryside is notorious for the clouds of venomous mosquitoes which it breeds.

The leader of Finland's ruling Social Democratic Party, when

I first went there after the war, was a tall young man who had fought against the Soviets in the famous Winter War. When I asked him if he knew any Russian, he replied: 'Only two words: hands up!'

I was particularly attracted by the Lapps, who spread across the mountains of Scandinavia close to the Arctic Circle. They make their living by herding reindeer and fishing, and still wear their attractive traditional costumes.

Denmark today owes much more to Hans Andersen than to its Viking ancestors. It has a quiet, gentle landscape. Copenhagen has one of the best city parks I know, and its harbour holds a lovely statue of Andersen's 'Little Mermaid'.

Laplander

Reindeer herd in Lapland

Eastern Europe

When the Second World War ended, the Red Army occupied the whole of Europe east of a line running from Stettin on the Baltic Sea to Trieste on the Adriatic. As International Secretary of the Labour Party, I went many times to eastern Europe, in the hope of helping the Social Democratic Parties to resist Soviet pressure for a merger with the Communist Party. It was a hopeless task, since when political pressure was insufficient, the Russians could rely on the KGB and the Red Army to assist them – as they did in Hungary in 1956.

I was personally very directly involved with the Polish Social Democratic Party. I had served with the Polish army in Italy for several months before the attack on Ancona. I returned to Poland in 1959, soon after Gomulka had asserted Poland's independence of the Soviet Union. The country was in a ferment of cultural freedom, although the political situation was still tightly controlled by the Polish Communist Party. Blood is far thicker than water in Poland. During a visit to the medieval capital, Cracow, I went to a concert given by the pianist Malcuzynski to celebrate the return of the crown jewels to the old royal castle of Wawel. Under the tattered banners of forgotten wars sat the three aristocracies of modern Poland – the ancient nobility, the new Communist élite and the Catholic hierarchy. They dissolved into tears together as, hectic with influenza, Malcuzynski played the great heroic *Polonaises*.

One day I went from Cracow to the concentration camp at

Band, Cracow

Auschwitz, which has been preserved in its wartime state. Walking round those deserted barracks in the snow was the most searing experience of my life. The most moving thing in Auschwitz is not the piles of human hair and teeth which were taken from the corpses in the gas chambers to contribute to the Nazi war effort, but wall upon wall of identity photographs of all the men, women and children who died there, as they were before arrest.

The city of Warsaw had been completely destroyed during the war. It was rebuilt by the Russians, whose Palace of Culture was detested by the Poles. They used to joke that the best view of Warsaw

Cathedral, Cracow

Market in Cracow, 1959

was from the top of the Palace of Culture, because it was the only place from which you could not see the Palace of Culture.

Daniel Defoe's poem on the Poles is still true two centuries later :

Uncommon monstrous virtues they posses,
Strange odd prepost'rous Polish qualities;
Mysterious contraries they reconcile,
The pleasing frown and the destroying smile;
Precisely gay, and most absurdly grave,
Most humbly high, and barbarously brave;
Debauch'dly civil and profanely good,
And filled with gen'rous brave ingratitude.

Hungary had spent most of the war in alliance with Nazi Germany. When I first went there in January 1947, young soldiers from the Red Army in pointed fur caps stood guard on the snowy runway when I landed from Vienna. Little had yet been done to repair the destruction caused by war. Rakosi, its Communist leader, had been in prison for fifteen years before the war and was an important member of the Comintern. A small, fat, bald man with the face of a Mongolian torturer, he told me jovially that he had joined the Fabian Society as an émigré in London before the Great War. Yet his Communist successors were to show nobility and courage in fighting Soviet power in 1956. It used to be said that a Hungarian is a man who can go into a revolving door behind you and come out in front.

Budapest, Hungary's capital city, has some beautiful buildings, particularly the castle overlooking the River Danube. The countryside

Castle in Budapest

Edna at Budva

to the south is beautiful, especially round the lovely Lake Balaton.

Yugoslavia is equally beautiful, particularly the lakes among the mountains in the north, and the towns on the coast to the south such as Budva and Dubrovnik. Yet politically it has no natural unity, having been put together artificially at the end of the First World War and combining Croats, Serbs, Montenegrins and Hungarians in the Vojvodina.

My first contact with Yugoslavia came during the Second World War when I was stationed at Bari on the Adriatic coast of southern Italy. Bari served as a base from which we helped the resistance in Yugoslavia through friends of mine such as Fitzroy McLean and Bill Deakin. As I have already mentioned, when the German forces in Italy surrendered at the beginning of May 1945, I decided to make a final 'swan' and to get, if possible, into Austria and Yugoslavia. At the frontier, the badge of our Sixth Armoured Division was planted above a cluster of German soldiers, all armed. When I called at the Divisional HQ I found my friend from Oxford, Tony Crosland, slim and handsome in his parachutist's beret. He told me our forward troops were in Klagenfurt. So on I went.

Among the hordes of refugees there were now individual German soldiers who had simply decided to walk home. The ditches were full of helmets, webbing and weapons, abandoned as they tried to lighten their load. In Klagenfurt I stayed with a platoon of the Rifle Brigade. Going over in the dark to the local *gasthaus* to brew some tea, I was met by a worried Special Forces officer in a jeep. He said that there were 2,000 armed Croat/Ustachis, allied with the Germans, milling around in the Adolf Hitler Platz, and that Tito's troops were infiltrating into the south of the town. Fortunately, there was not a major battle at that time. The Special Forces officer turned out to be a friend from Florence – Peter Wilkinson – whose account of his adventures in the resistance is described in his book, *Foreign Friends*. He later became our ambassador in Vienna.

The next day I went over a high pass into territory controlled by the partisans. Yugoslav forces were now in every village, so the situation in Trieste was extremely tense, since the political future of the area had not yet been decided. West of Trieste I passed through one of Tito's divisions on the march – a band of tough, ragged men, women and boys, all armed with captured weapons or British Sten guns, wearing every type of clothing, but all wearing the partisan grey forage cap with the red star.

After the war, Edna and I went on holiday to Yugoslavia, camping with our little children. One afternoon when I went for milk to the local farm, I was met by an old man still wearing his Austrian army greatcoat. I never met Tito myself, although I came to know one of his commanders well, Milovan Djilas, after he emigrated to Britain. He was an intellectual of great foresight.

Dubrovnik

Russia and Georgia

When I was a schoolboy in Bradford, my fascination with Russia began. Besides reading stories by Tolstoy, whom I still regard as the world's greatest writer of fiction, I also saw a production of Chekhov's *The Cherry Orchard* at the Bradford Civic Theatre by Komisajevsky, a refugee from Russia who had worked at the Arts Theatre in Moscow. I also saw at the Bradford Film Club a film by Eisenstein, *The General Line*, about a collective farm in Russia, which excited me so much that when I returned home I tried to write out the whole scenario shot by shot. Later I read Dostoevsky's *The Brothers Karamazov*, which presents the whole of Freudian theory through the three brothers: Dmitri represents the id, Ivan the ego, and Alyosha the super-ego. I loved Pushkin, whose poems were the basis of some of the greatest Russian operas – above all, Tchaikovsky's *Eugene Onegin*.

In 1959 I paid my first visit to Russia in a parliamentary delegation with Hugh Gaitskell and Nye Bevan. Edna and Dora Gaitskell came with us. The Kremlin symbolised the post-war Soviet Union with its mixture of superb medieval churches and ordinary modern government buildings inside an impregnable wall. Yet, our most vivid impression was of the warm emotional nature of the Russian people. Edna found it difficult to engage in a conversation with a Russian woman for more than a few minutes without the lady dissolving into tears on her shoulder – not from sorrow but from depth of feeling. The children in the schools we visited were straight out of

Inside the Kremlin

Summer Palace
of Peter the Great

a novel by Turgenev. The theatre and ballet had changed little since the Revolution, but they were of course among the best in the world. One thing which impressed us greatly on that visit was the number of young Chinese men and women in every factory and institute of learning. The Russians were deeply impressed – and not a little alarmed – by how hard they worked. On the last day of our visit, Macmillan called the general election in Britain.

My next visit to Russia was in 1963. There was not a Chinese to be seen since the break between Krushchev and Mao had taken place. I was able to have long talks with two of Russia's most distinguished 'bourgeois Jewish cosmopolitans': Ilya Ehrenburg, the novelist, and Ivan Maisky – a sad figure, desperate for news of Britain where he had greatly enjoyed his time as ambassador. He was fascinated by anything I could tell him of Israel.

In February 1984 I went to Moscow yet again, with Margaret Thatcher, David Owen and David Steel, for the funeral of Andropov. He had been head of the KGB yet was more liberal than most who preceded him. I found the KGB agents in Britain my best informants. They were usually disguised as journalists or diplomats but because they were not frightened of the KGB, they could talk with exceptional objectivity about what was happening in Russia.

In November 1984, I went to Moskow again with Neil Kinnock – we were both allowed to take our wives. For the first time I was able to visit Leningrad and found it quite fascinating. Because it looks across the sea, it is to Moscow what Shanghai is to Beijing or Hamburg to Bonn. Its people suffered appalling privations during the siege of 1941-3, yet the Russians restored Peter the Great's summer palace outside the city after its total destruction by the Germans. As well as the series of golden cascades which descend from the palace to the

Overleaf:
Gum Department Store, Red Square

Gulf of Finland below, the gardens are full of the trick fountains adored by Peter the Great, which squirt water on you if you sit on a particular seat or stand on a particular stone.

By this time the Stalinist prejudice against religion had ended. We went to the beautiful monastery of Novo Dievichi near Moscow and met a group of schoolgirls who were laying flowers at the grave of Krushchev and his wife. The following year I went with George Robertson (now Secretary General of NATO) to the celebrations of the

Red Army Day in Moscow

Model in Red Square

fortieth anniversary of Victory in Europe. We were less interested in the parade itself, impressive though it was, than in the freedom with which children were allowed to climb all over the tanks once they were stationary. We also went to Gorky Park, where the liberation of the Russian people was even more evident – it was just like Hyde Park on a Bank Holiday.

In 1986 I went yet again with a parliamentary delegation led by Willie Whitelaw, Mrs Thatcher's Deputy Prime Minister. We went to the beautiful medieval city of Zagorsk – outside Moscow, the most important centre of the Russian Orthodox Church. The same day we were given some insight into the government's road to heaven when we visited Star City where Soviet astronauts are trained. To our surprise we were allowed to photograph everything except the interior of the latest Mir space station.

Most interesting of all were our few days in Georgia – I had never before been outside European Russia. Georgia had been an independent state until its conquest by the Tsars in the nineteenth century, and it returned to independence for a short time after the Bolshevik Revolution. Living standards were higher in its capital, Tiflis, than in Moscow and lifestyles were far more easygoing. It is significant that Gorbachev himself comes from Stavropol, nearby on the northern foothills of the Caucasus. In the hills around Tiflis we visited several beautiful monasteries. Russia's nineteenth-century wars in the Caucasus have been well documented by some of her novelists such as Tolstoy and Lermontov. However, recent events have perhaps made the most interesting book Tolstoy's *Hadji Murad* about a war with the Chechens. It was one of the very last books he wrote, at the beginning of the twentieth century.

Israel and the Near East

My first visit to the Near East was in 1954, when I was invited to spend a fortnight in Israel by the Labour Party, Mapai. Israel was then only six years old, and half the country was a gigantic building site. New towns and villages were sprouting up everywhere to house the flood of immigrants, half of whom were from Russia and backward parts of Asia and Africa, particularly the Yemen. They spoke fifty-two different languages, spanning the whole range of the world's cultures and customs. The Yemenis had lived in a medieval Arab environment for over a thousand years, and the younger Russians had spent their whole lives under a Communist dictatorship.

Israel contains some major shrines both of the Muslim religion and of the three main Christian faiths, as well as of Jewry — a stupendous cultural inheritance which has been a political misfortune. The natural beauty of Lake Galilee and the Mount of Olives still has a luminous quality.

I recall the American delegate to the United Nations in 1946 appealing to the Jews and Arabs to behave like Christians. But the Christians did not set a good example in Palestine itself. Because the Catholic, Protestant and Orthodox churches could not agree on which of them should look after the most holy shrine in Christendom, the Church of the Holy Sepulchre in Jerusalem, they had to appoint an Arab caretaker.

Mount of Olives

I made some friends for life among the leaders of Mapai. I was most impressed by a young man in the Defence Ministry called Shimon Peres. He reminded me very much of the young Gaullists I had met at Strasbourg; this was not at all surprising since Peres' main responsibility at that time was to secure arms supplies from France. The Director of President Ben Gurion's office was an old friend from my days at Transport House, Teddy Kollek, who had spent some years in London as unofficial ambassador of Mapai. After independence he served for a time as Ben Gurion's private secretary before becoming Mayor of Jerusalem. The Director of the Foreign Office was the small and dapper Walter Eytan, who had in my time been a don at Queen's

Tel Aviv 1953

Lake of Galilee

College, Oxford, when his name was Ettinghausen. His colleague from Cambridge was Abba Eban. The Prime Minister of Israel was Golda Meir, whom I had first met in 1947 when she was leading the American Zionists and still called herself Goldie Myerson. The Socialist International was then meeting in Zurich just after the tragic incident of the Exodus – a boat full of Jewish refugees which had been stopped by the Royal Navy on its way to Palestine. As a young man of twenty-nine I had to debate this with one of the most formidable women in the world. She had a walkover. Later I met Israel's two leading generals, Yigal Alon and Moshe Dayan, who had been leaders in Israel's war for national identity. Dayan had lost an eye in the fighting. During the Profumo Affair, Golda Meir was asked what she would do if she found one of her military leaders was committing adultery. She replied, 'I would just knock out his other eye'.

Later I visited Jordan, then ruled by King Hussein. It acted as a buffer between Israel and the rest of the Arab world. The ancient Nabatean town of Petra is one of the wonders of the world – 'a rose-

Israeli girl

Petra, Jordan

red city half as old as time'. Jordan had at that time to depend on foreign aid to survive, since it was an unwilling host to a million Arab refugees from Israel. I found Syria less attractive, although its capital, Damascus, has some superb ancient temples.

Its geographical position has always given Turkey many problems. It is a bridge between south-east Europe and Asia Minor, with Iran and the old Soviet Union on its eastern frontier, Iraq and Syria to the south, Bulgaria and Greece to the west. In the period of Ottoman rule, Turkey's empire spread from Hungary to the Euphrates, including the Balkans and the bulk of the Middle East and North Africa. By the 1920s it no longer had foreign possessions and was able to join the western world. Its Aegean coast is covered with the ruins of the Ancient Greek civilisation. Indeed, well over a million Greeks were still living there until 1924, when they were brutally expelled. Its old capital, Istanbul, has some magnificent churches from ancient Byzantium. When I was there with NATO's Nuclear Planning Group, the Turkish government arranged a full turnout of the old Imperial Band in costumes and armour dating from Renaissance times. The fishing villages along the Bosphorus are extremely attractive. I particularly loved the hills and mountains facing the Aegean Sea, with a wealth of beautiful flowers in springtime.

Imperial Band in Istanbul

The Middle East

My name is Ozymandias, king of kings:
Look on my works, ye Mighty, and despair!
Shelley, 'Ozymandias', 1819

The Suez crisis led me into a preoccupation with the politics of the Middle East. As a result I was invited to make an extensive tour of the Arab countries and Iran at Easter 1960. It was a stunning experience. I started at the south of the Gulf in the little sheikhdom of Abu Dhabi.

Sheikh Shakhbut lived in a palace which was like a Beau Geste fort, with a scattering of palm trees and wattle huts nearby. When I visited his son, Prince Sultan, in the palace, I sat on a low cushion and was served with fragrant tea by a negro slave. Then the Prince leaned forward and asked me for the latest news of Nye Bevan's illness. The British agent's house, in which I stayed, was one of the few concrete buildings in Abu Dhabi at the time. Now Abu Dhabi is like Miami — a jungle of white skyscrapers.

I spent that Easter holiday in Iran at Isfahan, a city as beautiful as Florence, in a landscape as lovely as Tuscany — the grass a vivid green, the apple trees foaming with blossom and everything bursting into leaf. The air was icy clear under a brilliant sun, the blue sky patterned with fleecy clouds. The people were worthy of the landscape — above all the children, with great lustrous black eyes, cheeks the colour of a russet pippin and jet black hair; they wore tunics and trousers of multi-coloured cotton.

The climax of this expedition to Elysium was a journey from

Sheikh's Palace, Abu Dhabi

Temple in Isfahan

Qashgai migration

Shiraz to Persepolis through the middle of the Qashgai migration. The Qashgai at that time were a tribe of half a million people with 3 million camels, sheep, goats, donkeys and dogs; they travelled 500 miles for pasture every spring, from the shores of the Gulf into the mountains of central Persia, and back again in the autumn. As my taxi climbed over the pass, we were engulfed in a vast sea of Qashgai, gorgeous in their gypsy raiment, striding or riding towards Persepolis. The contrast between the lonely columns of Persepolis and the vulgar

mediocrity of the Sassanid tombs nearby was an object lesson in cultural decline. A thousand years later the same area had produced the great civilisation of the Muslim world, which stretched from Spain to the Moghul Empire of the Indian subcontinent. The mosques I visited, particularly the Friday Mosque in Isfahan, are among the greatest monuments of religious art in the world.

At that time there were no grand hotels in Isfahan, only a modest inn by the river run by a Swiss family, where I stayed. When I returned to Iran fifteen years later I found that the migration had ceased and the Qashgai themselves had been decimated by the Shah's

Ctesiphon

government, although I did see one or two in the bazaars of Shiraz.

My two visits to Iraq were far less agreeable. The first was during the rule of Colonel Qasim, a half-crazed dictator who kept his blood-stained shirt in a glass case in the room where I met him, as a reminder that an attempt to assassinate him had failed – Saddam Hussein had been one of the would-be assassins. The hospitals were full of men and women whose noses and ears had been cut off during the fighting in Kurdistan.

The Hanging Gardens of Babylon require a well trained imagination to convert their sewer-like trenches into one of the Seven Wonders of the Ancient World, although the reconstructions of Babylonian buildings are beautiful at dusk. What did surprise me with its grandeur was the ruined palace of Ctesiphon in the desert outside Baghdad – a gigantic vault of clay bricks, with a blind beggar singing epic songs to the music of a medieval instrument in the sand below.

When I first visited Saudi Arabia as Chancellor of the Exchequer, I was struck most of all by the honesty and dedication of the young top officials with whom I had to deal. They were fired by a sense of mission the equal of which I had met nowhere else in the Arab world. On one of my visits to Saudia Arabia I spent two days in the Hadramaut, a fertile valley sunk below the desert in a canyon about 300 miles from Aden. Life has changed little there in the last 2,000 years and until Freya Stark visited it some seventy years ago it had been almost inaccessible to western travellers. Its three towns, Shibam, Tarim and Sayun, all consist of lofty buildings made entirely of mud; the more prosperous are whitewashed. Sweet water abounds in the valley and many of the houses have one room flooded to a depth of about four feet. The water is used for bathing in the afternoons and flows out to irrigate the surrounding gardens. Edna and I slept on the

Overleaf: Shibam, Hadramaut

roof of the British agent's house in Tarim, where we watched the sun climb over the canyon wall in the pearly dawn, slowly raising the air temperature to furnace heat. The men of the Hadramaut are great sailors who have voyaged regularly over the centuries to Indonesia in search of trade and wives. The coast of Arabia must have been a rude shock to these Indonesian women, used to the lush vegetation of their islands, and the valley of the Hadramaut a blessed relief after over a hundred miles' journey through rocky desert.

As Defence Secretary I visited our base in Aden several times. The noise and stench of its crowded slums made it difficult to believe that its marriage with the surrounding sheikhdoms could survive. The Adenis were overwhelmingly for Nasser and the Arab League. Even in the sheikhdoms most of the schoolteachers were Egyptian nationalists. One of them had married the local sheikh. Her first act was to get her headmaster executed. However, I was greatly impressed by the top British officials in the area. Sir Charles Johnson, the Governor of Aden on my first visit, was a languid cynic married to Natasha Bagratian, a descendant of the royal family which ruled Georgia before it was taken over by the Czars. Together they produced an excellent translation into Byronic stanzas of *Eugene Onegin*. Sir Richard Turnbull, a later Governor, looked like a pernickety schoolmaster but was a tough administrator. He told me that when the British Empire finally sank beneath the waves of history, it would leave behind it only two monuments: one was the game of Association Football, the other was the expression 'fuck off'.

Tarim, Hadramaut

Egypt and North Africa

The state of Egypt came into existence 3,000 years before the birth of Christ. It soon became a major power in the ancient world. Ninety pyramids were built as burial places for its kings, the most famous of whom was Tutankhamun, who was born at Luxor in the fourteenth century BC. In his time, Egypt had a great cultural influence in the eastern Mediterranean, particularly on Crete. In the last three centuries BC, Egypt was ruled by the Ptolemy dynasty (of whom the last was Queen Cleopatra), then by the Muslims, the Turks and finally the British, who annexed Egypt in 1882. The country achieved independence after the First World War.

Its present capital, Cairo, is nowadays overpopulated, noisy and polluted, but contains some ancient monuments as notable as any, particularly the beautiful mosque of Ibn Tulun, while the pyramids of Giza are on its outskirts.

I visited Egypt several times as Defence Secretary and came to know its then leader, Colonel Nasser, well. He was then worshipped as the greatest hero of his time from the Atlantic to the Indian Ocean. In a mud village outside the mighty Sassanid ruins at Ctesiphon, in Iraq, I heard bands of young men chanting his name to the sound of a drum and shouting 'Long live Arabism'. I later saw his colour photograph among the spices and boiled sweets in the soukhs of the Hadramaut. The Arab governments, however, took a very different view. Nuri Said of Iraq was Nasser's sworn enemy. He was feared and hated by the kings and princes of Saudi Arabia and the Gulf.

Nasser was a large, handsome man of great ability and charm, yet

Sphinx and Pyramid

Overleaf: Cairo

170

his judgement was poor. He grossly over-extended Egyptian power in the Middle East. His union with Syria never made political or economic sense.

While in Egypt, I tried without success to see the temples of Abu Simbel before they were moved to escape the rising waters of the Nile, but I did watch the building of the Aswan Dam. It was a task comparable with the building of the pyramids.

I also paid several visits to Libya, which under King Idris had good

River Nile

Ibn Tulun, Cairo

relations with Britain. It was obvious that the monarchy was likely to fall at any moment to an army coup, and I tried to guess which of the young colonels I met was most likely to lead it. In the end I decided it would probably be Colonel Shelhi, an intelligent young man who was said to be influenced by Nasser. I was wrong, but not very wrong. Shortly after Colonel Qaddafi had taken over I was told by our ambassador that Shelhi had been woken by his batman on the morning of the coup with the words: 'Excuse me, sir, the revolution

has begun'. 'Don't be silly,' was his reply, 'it's tomorrow.'

During the Second World War, I spent several weeks in Algeria and Tunisia with Britain's First Army, racing along the coast from Algiers to Tunis before landing in Sicily and taking part in the Italian campaign. Our camp at Bougie on the coast had a true feel of North Africa. I described the scene in my diary:

Grasshoppers whirred away like cotton looms. Nearer a big cicada was tirelessly creaking. Down in the valley a donkey brayed his eternal protest, Punchinello on all fours. The sea was emerald, stained with violet and ochre. Two slender masts projected through its surface beyond the harbour. By a berth a couple of ships lay on their sides embracing one another. High over the port the silver bees were poised, forever motionless on their invisible wires. Behind, a hedge of cactus hid an Arab farm, enclosing a tiny patio where naked babies crawled among the flies and dirt. Pink, saffron, black and scarlet flared in the stone fields below a pool of yellow flowers – it was a woman doubled under a load of hay.

Our Mediterranean idyll came to an end on the scorching beach at Hammamet, where we were drawn up in a square to hear an inspirational address from General Montgomery. He did not impress us with his sharp, ferret-like face and pale grey-green eyes, wearing his vanity like a foulard.

Mosque of Sheikh Muhammed

Africa

In 1962 I visited the Congo during the civil war. I had been to black Africa before, and was quite unprepared for the dull skies and soggy damp of the western coastlands. I was disappointed too, by the absence of big game, though while having tea with our minister in Leopoldville I saw a green mamba hanging from a branch above my seat.

On the other hand, I found the African people immensely impressive. The men I met were intelligent and dedicated to making independence work. In Ghana the women ran the country's commercial life. Their clothing differed according to their tribe or country far more than that of the men; in Nigeria the Yoruba women wore bright-blue turbans and dresses, while the Wolof women in Dakar wore silks and gauze in the styles of the French second empire. I paid a visit to a tribal chief, the Alafin of Oyo, near Ibadan in western Nigeria. My arrival in his compound was heralded by tom-toms and I sat on one of his many thrones as we talked; his favourite throne was a dentist's chair. Oyo had a custom which might well be copied elsewhere. When the elders feel that the Alafin is not up to his job, they send him a bowl of parrot's eggs and he takes his own life.

Later that year Edna and I represented the Labour Party at the celebrations of independence in Uganda. The contrast with western Africa was surprising. Instead of louring clouds over a tropical rain forest, we found dazzling skies over rolling hills planted with tea and

Yoruba woman, Nigeria

Overleaf:
Fishermen in the Congo

Nigerian girls

coffee and a multitude of wild animals. We spent two days at the magnificent Queen Elizabeth Game Park, where the blue peaks of Ruwenzori hang over scrubland teeming with elephants, hippopotomuses, cheetahs and every sort of deer, monkey and tropical bird.

In September 1970, I spent a week in South Africa as a guest of the National Union of South African Students, who were strongly opposed to apartheid. By 11.30 on the morning of my arrival, after travelling all night, I was off on a journey of 550 miles by car into the heart of Zululand with Steve Biko, who was later murdered in jail.

Because I had been Defence Secretary and could be expected to value the Royal Navy's base at Simonstown, the government in Pretoria accepted my request that I should be allowed to visit Nelson Mandela in prison on Robben Island. There was no chance of escape. The island was surrounded by rocks and seaweed; the water was very cold and the currents strong enough to sweep any swimmer out to sea. I walked round the island, which was uninhabited outside the prison. It was like a tiny Garden of Eden, in which rabbits and guinea fowl, which had never seen a man, played unfrightened among arum lilies, wattle and a profusion of wild flowers. I had met Mandela only once before, when a friend of my army days in Italy introduced us during one of his clandestine visits to London. When I saw him in September 1970 he was fifty-two, a few months younger than I, and had already been a prisoner for over eight years. Today we rightly see him as one of the outstanding figures in the world.

Elsie's River, South Africa

India

I had many friends from India when I was a student – Indira Ghandi was an undergraduate while I was at Balliol. After the war most of my friends went into government or the diplomatic service. Yet although I often passed through Bombay and Calcutta on my way to the Far East, I did not pay my first proper visit to India until 1992, with Edna.

We were captivated by the beauty of the countryside and the people – above all, by the colour of the women's clothing. India's temples, forts and palaces reflect its turbulent history, particularly the conflict between the Muslim and Hindu traditions. Yeats presents the Muslim tradition perfectly with the words:

A starlit or a moonlit dome disdains
All that man is,
All mere complexities,
The fury and the mire of human veins.

while he describes the Hindu culture with the words:

Caught in that sensual music, all neglect
Monuments of unageing intellect.

Delhi, like most capital cities, is noisy and overcrowded, although its Red Fort and Friday Mosque are well worth a visit. The greatest

Fortress Palace of Amber

Hashish seller

Taj Mahal from Red Fort

beauties of India, however, are at least a 100 miles away to the south. In the sixteenth century, the Mughal Emperors decided to make Agra their capital. Akbar built the magnificent riverside fort of red sandstone; a hundred years later Shah Jahan built the world's greatest monument, the Taj Mahal, as a mausoleum for his beloved wife. About 150 miles to the west is Jaipur, remarkable for its pink buildings and multitude of monkeys. In the eighteenth century, its ruler Jai Singh II, a great admirer of Newton, built an extraordinary collection of geometrical objects in one of his gardens to enable him to pursue his astronomical interests. Just outside Jaipur is the beautiful fortress

Meherangarh

palace of Amber overlooking a lake. Edna and I rode up to it on the back of an elephant. The walls of its interior shine with powdered marble and even pearls, and some of the apartments are encrusted with coloured mirror glass set in patterns.

Jodhpur is an exceptionally dry city on the edge of the Thar Desert. Just outside is the great fort of Meherangarh. There are beautiful desert villages to the east of Jodhpur where Edna and I were able to eat cross-legged in a tent with the local rajah. I drank a little

opium from the cupped hand of my host; however, it seemed to have no effect whatever. The fort at Gwalior stands on a massive rock and is approached by passing colossal Jain statues from the seventh to the fifteenth centuries: they are curiously reminiscent of Greek *kouroi*. We found Udaipur the most beautiful place in Rajasthan. On the edge of Pichola Lake there are not only a superb city palace but also the best gardens in India, where fountains play over lotus pools, marble kiosks and life-size marble elephants. We found the Lake Palace Hotel on a tiny island in the lake, perhaps the most beautiful place we have ever stayed. Remarkably, I had met one of its managers in Leeds! About sixty miles from Udaipur we saw the Jain temple of Ranakpur, made even lovelier by the coloured clothes of its Indian visitors.

We ended our visit to India by going to Bombay so that we could cross to the small island of Elephanta. The fascinating sculptures of its rock-cut temples were much damaged by the Portuguese. We found the rocky path up the hill to see them so overcrowded by tourists and touts that the visit was hardly worthwhile.

Temple of Ranakpur

South-East Asia

My first visit to South-East Asia was in early June 1964. It taught me invaluable lessons for my job as Defence Secretary, which started a month later. In Vietnam I was taken by the Americans in a helicopter gunship to positions in the Mekong Delta, where the fighting was fiercest. By their excessive use of air power and the indiscriminate slaughter of civilians on the ground, the Americans turned the whole population of Vietnam against them. Despite sending up to half a million troops to Vietnam, they lost the war.

In Borneo on the other hand, during the war of confrontation with Indonesia, the British Director of Operations, General Walter Walker, knew that the key to victory would be winning the hearts and minds of the local people. The frontier ran across mountains and marshes, in dense forest and jungle. There were no roads. The helicopter was king; a battalion with six helicopters was worth a brigade with none. Most useful of all were units of the Special Air Service (SAS) and its marine equivalent, the Special Boat Service. The commander of 22 SAS, Lieutenant Colonel John Woodhouse, was a diffident, unmilitary figure in rumpled khaki, who might have been a botanist. He was, by common consent among the few who knew his record, the greatest expert in guerrilla warfare yet produced by the West – a man to compare with Ho Chi Minh. When I became Secretary of State for

Above: the Mekong Delta

Overleaf: by the river in Saigon

Dance in Longhouse, Borneo

Defence the following month, I would not allow the use of bombers in Borneo. As a result, in four years of fighting the British never once dropped a bomb from an aircraft. Thus there were fewer casualties in the whole campaign than are caused by road accidents on an average Bank Holiday weekend in Britain. And we won.

I visited our troops in Borneo as often as I could, flying by helicopter to little wooden forts on the frontier, from which our troops organised their jungle patrols high on the ridge of blue romantic mountains with names like Bukit Nukel, or by a muddy river surrounded by monkeys, iguanas and crocodiles.

Edna was with me when we flew to a small longhouse on the upper reaches of the Limbang River. There we drank *tuak* — a potent mixture of cider with honey and gin. A rifle was fired and a cock waved over our libations before we embarked on longboats made of hollowed-out tree trunks and powered by outboard motors, for a two-hour journey down the river and over the rapids. We disembarked at another longhouse. After drinking more *tuak*, we were made to join in the sword dancing; it was quite an ordeal after so much alcohol in the boiling heat.

Edna performed so well that the head man gestured for a large rope net to be lowered from the rafters. Out of it rolled a number of small wicker baskets about the size of small melons. The head man picked one out and presented it to Edna. It contained the head of a Japanese solider, perfectly preserved by being hung in the smoke of a fire. On returning to London we declared the head to the Customs as an anthropological specimen. It lay in a plastic bag behind the sofa in our bedroom at Admiralty House until found by a woman cleaner, who took a long time to recover.

I paid regular visits to our base in Hong Kong. Its main purpose was to prevent illegal immigration from the mainland, which was not easy. Our British and Gurkha battalions were too few to cope with the hundreds of thousands of Chinese peasants who were liable to flood across the land frontier when there was a famine anywhere nearby. There had been such a tidal wave shortly before I became Defence Secretary. When the Japanese were defeated in 1945, the Chinese population was under a million. It had risen to 4 million by the time I left office in 1970, creating formidable housing problems. It is now over 10 million.

Hongkong Floating Market

Klongs Charcoal seller

Despite its shanty towns clinging precariously to the hillsides outside Kowloon, and the harbours littered with the floating villages in which a large part of its people still lived, Hong Kong was then a place of great beauty. The paddy fields where Hakka women planted rice wearing wide-brimmed hats with fringes of black cloth are now often replaced by shiny new cities of skyscrapers.

Since Bangkok was the capital of the South-East Asian Treaty Organisation, I paid several visits to Thailand. I had to get up at 5 in the morning to see the floating markets of the *klongs*, since I was

meeting the Prime Minister at eight.

The temples or wats in Bangkok are exceptionally beautiful, like inverted bells or wine glasses. As you walk round their terraces among Buddhist priests in their saffron robes, among life-size gilt statues of legendary birds with the bodies of women, it is difficult to believe that most of them are only a century old, and that their glittering multi-coloured surfaces consist of millions of pieces of broken crockery.

After the Second World War Britain's main base in the Far East was Singapore, which I visited many times. Its Prime Minister, Lee Kuan Yew, became a close friend. He had been the most brilliant schoolboy of his age in Singapore, as his wife, Choo, was the most brilliant schoolgirl. He took a double first in law at Cambridge; Choo also took a first there after only two years' study. Lee was brought up to speak English and learned Mandarin as well as Malay only when he entered politics. He is especially proud of being of the Hakka people, who originated in north China. The Hakka are the Prussians of China and there is a lot of the Prussian in Lee Kuan Yew. He believes in discipline and hard work. His rival, the Prime Minister of the Federation of Malaysia, was a Tunku, meaning prince. His pride in one of his ancestors, who was said to have been a vampire, led him to finance a film, *The King with Fangs*, out of which he made $100,000. Despite appearances, he was an able and cunning politician. He told me his simple rule: 'If you have an enemy you can defeat on your own, fight. If you have an enemy you can defeat with allies, fight. If your enemy is China, surrender.'

Buddhist Priests in Bangkok

China

China has fascinated me ever since I was bowled over as a boy by the exhibition of Chinese art in London. I had read Edgar Snow's classic account of the Long March, *Red Star Over China*, as an undergraduate. Malraux's novel about the suppression of the Communist revolt in Shanghai, *La Condition Humaine*, had made a lasting impressing on me during the war. So when Britain finally established limited relations with Peking in 1972 I made a point of getting to know the Chinese chargé d'affaires. My standing with Chinese diplomats greatly improved when they discovered that my daughter, Jenny, was teaching some of their children, and improved even more when they decided that her husband was a genuine member of the British proletariat; the Cultural Revolution was exceptionally snobbish in this respect.

We found the Chinese attractive and intelligent as individuals, with a very English sense of humour. There was no sense of an omnipresent secret police, which was so oppressive in the Soviet Union. Nor was there much sign of the armed forces; the few we did see all wore the same cotton uniforms, without insignia of rank, and were treated with no special respect by the crowds of civilians.

We followed the usual route for foreign visitors: political discussions in Peking; short trips to Shanghai, Hangchow and Nanking; visits to schools, factories and collective farms; sightseeing at the Great Wall and the Ming tombs; and evenings at the theatre to see acrobats or Chinese operas with propagandist themes.

Every moment was fascinating to us, from our first walk in the

Buddha in China

gardens outside the imperial palace, on the warm autumn afternoon when we arrived, to our final visit to a hospital, where we saw acupuncture anaesthesia used for procedures as varied as thyroidectomy, removal of a cartilage, female sterilisation and dentistry. Peking was a city of bicycles; there were very few cars. For the first time the regime was beginning to worry about environmental pollution, planting trees to control the omnipresent dust which blew in from the surrounding countryside. Dust was the reason why so many people wore gauze face-masks in the streets. In the hope of

Acupuncture anaesthesia

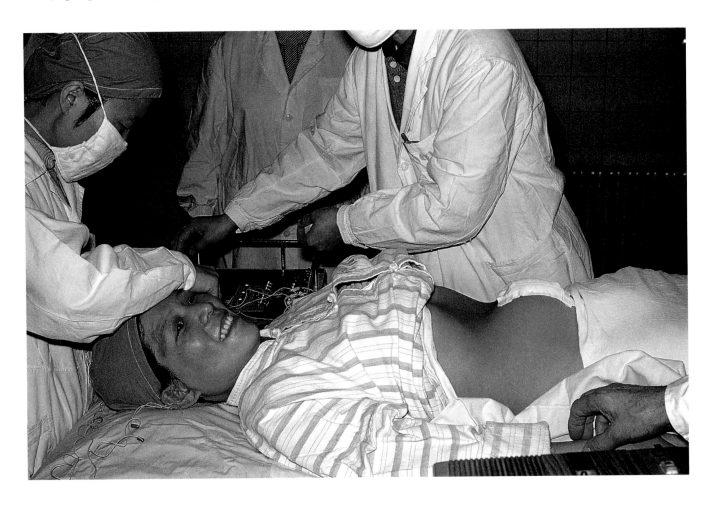

School science lesson

limiting the growth of China's population, marriages were discouraged before the age of twenty-five, and young men and women were not allowed even to hold hands in public.

The Cultural Revolution was then coming to an end. The only time we saw Mao's famous 'Little Red Book' was at the end of a political opera in Shanghai, when the whole cast advanced towards the audience waving it. When we visited the university in Peking, it still had only a third of its student complement, having reopened two years earlier after being closed for most of the Cultural Revolution.

Street in Peking

However, the Revolution was by no means ended, as we discovered when we visited a 'May 7th Cadre School' near Peking. Government servants were sent there for brainwashing: three months for the bureaucrats, six months for the teachers. To prevent officials from losing contact with the realities of peasant life, they were made to perform the most menial tasks available on the collective farm, while studying Communist theory in the evenings. We watched a headmistress trying to call her hens to order with her school whistle.

Typical of the thrust of the course was a systematic demonstration that ordure was a precious gift to agriculture, and not something dirty to be despised. One after another, the students got up and recited to us how they had been to clean out the latrines on their first day, and how awful the smell was. It would have been more impressive if they had not all spoken in the same lugubrious tones and used exactly the same words to describe their ordeal. I must confess that by the end Edna and I had the greatest difficulty in keeping our faces straight.

Fourteen years later I spent a few days in Peking again. There had been a social and economic revolution so complete that I felt a little nervous as to whether perhaps it had gone too far, too fast. The new men in power were not the products of the previous system, but its victims. But politically there was the same uniformity as before; no one was allowed to say a good word about the old days. And though I was delighted to find that young lovers could at last hold hands in the public parks, and that China was no longer a cultural desert, there were worrying signs that the new market economy was bringing corruption in its wake.

China has a land area larger than most continents, extending from the tropics almost to the Arctic Circle. Its many peoples differ as much in appearance from one another as Moors from Norwegians, and now number a thousand million. The oldest civilisation on Earth, China has monuments of great beauty. We saw the Forbidden City (which was the old Imperial Palace in Peking); the Great Wall, built to protect the frontier only fifty miles away against Mongol invasion; the tombs of the Ming emperors, and many ancient temples in the beautiful lake district around Hangchow. The Confucian tradition,

Red Army officers

Barefoot Doctors

which combines authoritarianism with pragmatism, is still influential in China. It lays great stress on conformity and team spirit. The Communists have added the cult of physical fitness; as we drove round the streets of Shanghai after sunrise, we saw people shadow-boxing on their way to work. It was a bit too much like an English public school. I came to the conclusion by the time I left China that it was a country of Wykhamists led by Balliol men.

We visited several 'people's communes'. Each family was allowed a little private allotment of its own, and the commune could sell surplus output freely after making its planned contribution to the official market. Health was largely the responsibility of the so-called 'barefoot doctors' – a corps of young men and women with minimal

Overleaf:
Observatory near Hangchow

medical training who travelled from commune to commune rather like parish priests. Many of the old men wore their beards long in the traditional style, their wives hobbling by their sides on feet deformed by the barbarous practice of binding which was common before the Revolution. The robust self-confidence of the children was a striking contrast. I was heavily defeated at ping-pong in the Children's Palace in Shanghai by an urchin only seven years old.

Hangchow Lake

Ming Statue

Japan

Even as a schoolboy I had loved the coloured prints of Hokusai, Hiroshige and Fujimoro. Later I read the novels of Mishima and loved the films of Kurosawa. Yet I saw little of this beauty during my first few days in Japan in 1964, when it was still suffering from the hangover of its post-war boom. Tokyo was a chaotic muddle and the surrounding countryside was like the wasteland between Liverpool and Manchester.

When I returned in 1979, Tokyo had flowery patios and leafy pedestrian precincts and compared favourably with most other great cities. The country was still grossly overpopulated and excessive protection for the rice farmers meant that far too little land was

Park in Kyoto

Geisha in Gion

available for the rest of the population. My Japanese friends still defined their three ambitions as 'Japanese wife, Chinese cooking and western-style house'. On a clear day you could still see the sacred mountain of Fuji from the heart of Tokyo. In many households the husband changed from his constricting western suit and shoes into a loose kimono and sandals as soon as he arrived home from work. When we visited a Shinto shrine we were given a piece of dry cake which stayed in my cupboard in England for many years.

Shinto is not so much a religion as a system of social and family

Musician in Kyoto

Mount Fuji

observances. Many Japanese are Buddhists as well as professing Shinto. The most beautiful temples are far from Tokyo in the ancient capitals of Nara and Kyoto. The great complex of buildings which forms the Todai-ji shrine outside Nara is scattered across a wooded hillside over which thousands of tame deer roam freely. Edna and I were taken to a tea house in Gion, a part of Kyoto which is the only place in Japan where geishas are still trained. We had a long talk with a girl of twenty who, after four years training as a Maiko'san, or apprentice geisha, was about to launch out on her own as a fully qualified member of the trade union. She was an intelligent and spirited girl of great independence, and looked forward to leaving the school and earning money for herself.

In Japan the garden is a major art form, of symbolic and religious significance as well as visual beauty. Even the most untrained western eye must see the Katsura garden as one of the most beautiful in the world, particularly in autumn when the maples are crimson and gold. It is the garden of a seventeenth-century Imperial palace, itself a unique architectural masterpiece in which squares and rectangles are assembled with classical precision, so as to set forms of abstract intellectual purity against the irregular and ever-changing shapes and colours of water, trees and sky.

Temple in Todai-ji

Katsura Gardens

The United States

I had many American friends at Oxford. Howard K. Smith, who later became a CBS correspondent in London, married a beautiful Danish girl called Benny, who had long legs, silky auburn hair and a milky complexion – the soldier's dream of a girl from *Esquire* magazine. Walt Rostow later became an adviser to several American Presidents. I met Henry Kissinger and Zbigniew Brzezinski, while they were still at Harvard – they also became advisors to the U.S. President. Jim King became Deputy Head of the CIA. Phil Kaiser became America's minister in London.

I wrote weekly articles for the *New Republic* and the *New Leader* until I became Defence Secretary in 1964. As a minister, I went to the United States as often as three times a year. I loved to search out the remnants of American history, particularly in colonial Williamsburg, which is preserved as it was 300 years ago thanks to the Rockefeller family; the local people still wear colonial dress and as far as possible carry on the trades of their ancestors.

In 1979, I went to a party given by Ken Galbraith and Arthur Schlesinger, who laid the foundations for the thinking of the Kennedy years. Though they were ten years apart in age, they celebrated their common birthday in 1979 and when I joined them I met the extraordinary aristocracy of American liberalism – Jimmy Wechsler, almost the only American ex-Communist with the courage to stand up to McCarthy; Lauren Bacall; Jackie Onassis; and Leonard

May Day in Washington

IN THIS TEMPLE
AS IN THE HEARTS OF THE PEOPLE
FOR WHOM HE SAVED THE UNION
THE MEMORY OF ABRAHAM LINCOLN
IS ENSHRINED FOREVER

Lincoln Memorial

Girl near San Francisco

Bernstein. I found Washington particularly lovely at Easter when Tidal Basin is a sea of cherry blossom.

San Francisco is the most attractive of all American cities, at least for a European. My younger daughter, Cressida, has been living there for the last thirty years. The Golden Gate Bridge is one of the wonders of the modern world. In 1966, when as Defence Secretary I was going round the world in ten days, I spent a night in San Francisco at a hotel where a noticeboard announced that there would be a performance that evening by a Mrs Spiegelbaum, 'the only topless mother of eight'.

Los Angeles is far less attractive – still a hundred suburbs in search of a city – and when I used to go there it suffered appallingly from smog. But just outside is the university town of Pasadena, with a superb art gallery which has the best collection of Degas drawings in the world.

The United States is unique for the beauty of its great national parks. The Grand Canyon is quite remarkable, standing as it does in the middle of a great desert, its rocks towering over a tiny stream below. My personal favourite is Yosemite, about 200 miles from San Francisco, a wooded valley surrounded by towering rocks from which waterfalls flow beautifully in the springtime when the snow is melting. I used to go to conferences at Aspen in Colorado, which is surrounded by the Rocky Mountains. Close to the border with Mexico is a town called Balboa, with its Tree of Life always crowded with little children.

Grand Canyon

El Capitan, Yosemite

Tree of Life in Balboa Park

The Caribbean and Mexico

My father spent two years just after the war in Barbados, organising technical education in the West Indies. He made friends there whom I often met myself in later life. I made my own first visit to the West Indies in 1975, as Chancellor of the Exchequer, for the Commonwealth Finance Ministers' Conference. We loved the dazzling white beaches of Barbados, and the contrast in Jamaica between the crime-ridden capital city of Kingston and the beautiful coast in the north, particularly Dunn's Falls, where cool fresh water fans over a series of mountain boulders on to the sand and sea – the setting for a hundred advertisements. Everywhere on the coast the dark green of the palms contrasts vividly with the dazzling white sand and the pale fiery turquoise of the sea itself.

I was fascinated by Guyana; the capital, Georgetown, had been laid out by the methodical Dutch in neat squares separated by canals, now choked by giant water lilies. The beautiful parks had large ponds among the palm trees in which you could see sea creatures called manatees which sailors used to mistake for mermaids.

The Caribbean hosts an extraordinary variety of languages and cultures from Europe, Africa and Asia. The European plantation colonies were manned by labourers from Africa and Asia who developed a unique Creole culture of their own, now reflected in their colourful carnivals.

Beach in Barbados

Dunn's Falls

In April 1978 I took my first meeting of the Interim Committee of the International Monetary Fund as Chairman in Mexico. The Mexican government wanted the meeting held in Acapulco to boost its tourist trade. President Carter thought this would give a bad impression to his Baptist supporters, so we held it in the noise and smog of Mexico City. I thought it a much more suitable location since my colleagues could not ignore the problems of the Third World when they were surrounded by unemployed peasants who had crowded into the city slums with their families from an even poorer countryside. Banditry was so common that the Mexican Central Bank had to distribute its currency round the country in its own fleet of

Jamaican prison

aircraft. After the meeting one of them flew us off to the stupendous Maya city of Chichen Itza. On the terraces of its great pyramids I found the reclining figure of the Rain God, *Chacmool*, which had inspired the young Henry Moore.

In Mexico City itself the Anthropological Museum's collection of ancient Mexican art rivals the treasures of Tutankhamun in Cairo. Mexico resembles Egypt in many other ways. It had been the centre of American culture 4,000 years before the Spanish conquered it at the beginning of the sixteenth century. Its Olmec civilisation coincided roughly with that of classical Greece, the Maya civilisation with that of the Roman Empire. The Toltec and Aztec civilisations coincided with that of Elizabethan England. It wasted a century in civil wars and was conquered by the United States, and France in succession. It finally achieved independence and order in 1920. In recent times it has probably been best known for its music and dancing – superbly represented by the exotic Carmen Miranda.

Market in Mexico City

Epilogue

Travel has been an important part of my life for over eighty years. Besides the pleasure I have enjoyed from the interest and beauty of the people and landscapes I have seen, I have learned some lessons. All over the world the people, like us, are human beings – but they are not human beings like us. Different landscapes tend to produce different people. Mountains and deserts, prairies and forests all help to shape their own types of people irrespective of nationality or language. The people of the Scottish Highlands often have more in common with those of the Alps or the Pyrenees than with those of Edinburgh.

So if you want to understand the nature – or even the politics – of a people, it is useful to meet them in their natural environment. I hope this book may help to increase the understanding of those who are unable to travel so widely themselves.